STEP-BY-STEP
GUITAR
MAKING

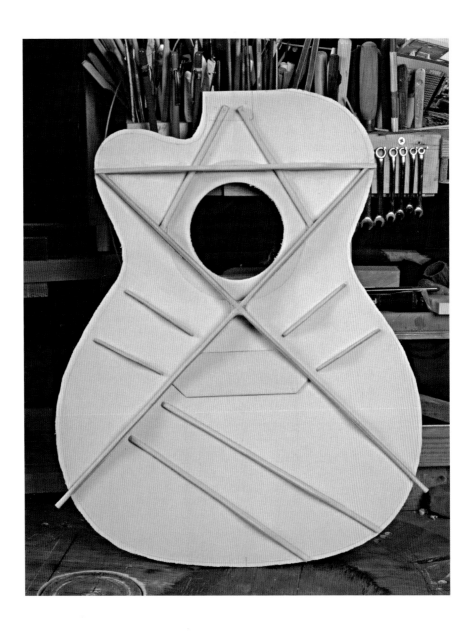

STEP-BY-STEP
GUITAR
MAKING

ALEX WILLIS

Publisher: Alan Giagnocavo

ISBN 978-1-56523-331-7

To learn more about the other great books from Fox Chapel Publishing, or to find a retailer near you, call toll-free 1-800-457-9112 or visit us at www.FoxChapelPublishing.com.

Note to Authors: We are always looking for talented authors to write new books in our area of woodworking, design, and related crafts. Please send a brief letter describing your idea to Peg Couch, Acquisition Editor, 1970 Broad Street, East Petersburg, PA 17520.

Printed in China
10 9 8 7 6 5 4 3 2 1

CONTENTS

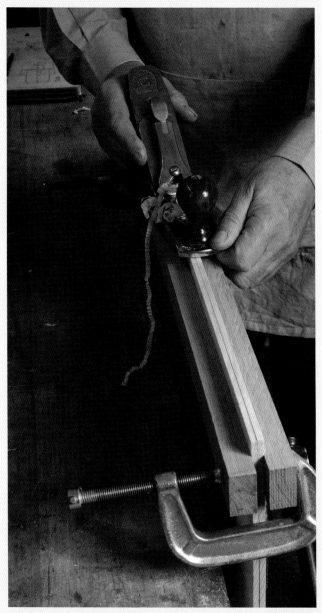

PART 2: GUITAR MAKING STEP BY STEP

INTRODUCTION

We have all admired beautiful handmade guitars in shops, or played by a favourite musician on stage. This book will show you how to make one yourself without breaking the bank. With basic woodworking skills, a small workshop and only a few specialist tools, you should be able to create a guitar fit for the concert platform.

The acoustic guitar featured in this book, and in the full-size plans provided at the back, is modelled on the famous OM (Orchestra Model) first made by C. F. Martin, with six steel strings, a cutaway, and 14 frets to the body joint. This model is well suited to the fingerstyle player, giving a well-balanced sound with good separation and sustain. The procedures used to make it are just as applicable to any other kind of flat-top guitar – that is, any guitar in which the soundboard is made from a flat piece of wood, as opposed to arch-top guitars which are carved from the solid.

There are some things you need to decide on before you start. Where will you build the guitar, and what tools will you need? What wood are you going to use? In the following chapters I will answer these questions and discuss the methods to be employed. Additional things to think about are what shape, size and scale length your guitar will be – though if you follow the plans provided, these questions will be answered for you.

The guitar described in this book uses Brazilian rosewood (*Dalbergia nigra*) for the back and ribs, Brazilian mahogany (*Swietenia macrophylla* or *S. mahagoni*) for the neck, Alpine spruce (*Picea abies*) for the soundboard, North American Sitka spruce (*Picea sitchensis*) for the bracing, and African ebony (*Diospyros crassiflora* or a related species) for the fretboard and bridge – so it is truly an international guitar. Brazilian rosewood is an endangered species, but mine was obtained from an ethical source: it is stump wood, reclaimed from tree stumps left behind from felling more than 50 years ago.

Well-made acoustic guitars are like fine wines: they need time to mature, and if taken care of and played regularly, they will develop subtleties in sound and tone that will bring enjoyment to both player and listener for many years to come.

This book is intended to give you all the information you require to construct your first guitar. With the skills you acquire in the process, you could, if you choose, go on to make other stringed instruments such as ukuleles, bouzoukis and mandolins. If you want a new challenge in life, you might even consider a career change – a chance to develop those creative skills that have been dormant until now. Starting a business making musical instruments is an exciting possibility; if it appeals to you, you would be wise to consult a qualified business adviser.

PART 1
PLANNING AND PREPARATION

GUITAR ANATOMY

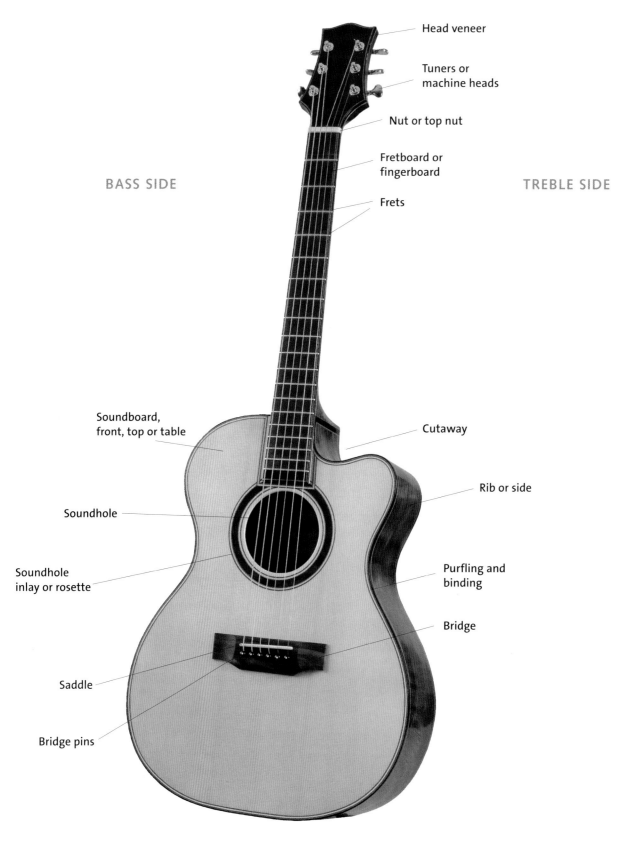

Head veneer

Tuners or machine heads

Nut or top nut

Fretboard or fingerboard

Frets

BASS SIDE

TREBLE SIDE

Soundboard, front, top or table

Cutaway

Soundhole

Rib or side

Soundhole inlay or rosette

Purfling and binding

Bridge

Saddle

Bridge pins

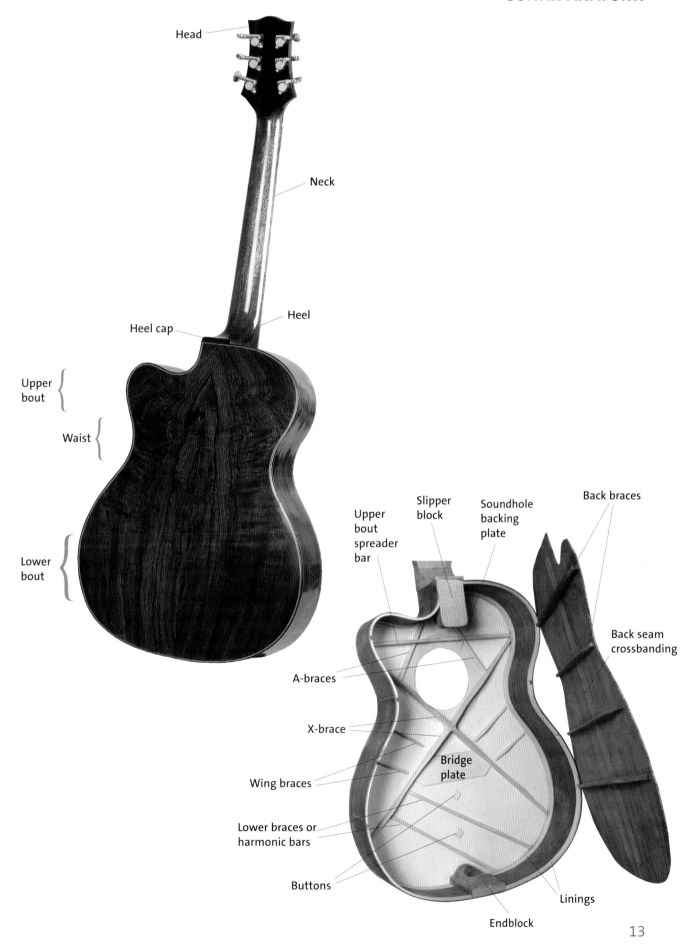

Head

Neck

Heel

Heel cap

Upper bout

Waist

Lower bout

Upper bout spreader bar

Slipper block

Soundhole backing plate

Back braces

A-braces

X-brace

Bridge plate

Back seam crossbanding

Wing braces

Lower braces or harmonic bars

Buttons

Linings

Endblock

13

TOOLS AND EQUIPMENT

My main workbench enjoys both natural and artificial light, and racks for the most-used hand tools are close by

This book is written on the assumption that you already have some experience in working with wood, and that you have a suitable area to work in, such as a shed or garage, and a basic set of woodworking tools. If you need any advice on basics such as tool use and sharpening, there are plenty of good books available that will set you on the right track.

As far as tools are concerned, the old adage that you get what you pay for is very true. It is best to invest in just the tools you need as you need them, and purchase the best quality you can afford. Special occasions such as birthdays are good times to drop hints to friends and family. There are excellent tool suppliers who offer free printed and online catalogues, and specialist luthiers' suppliers can provide those items which are not available from ordinary tool dealers. If money is tight, it is quite possible to devise home-made alternatives for many of these.

You will probably already have most of the tools you need, such as planes, chisels, gouges and the like. Some more specialized items that will be extremely useful are listed on the following pages. Substitutes for some of these tools are discussed in the relevant chapters.

Having bought good tools, look after them. Sweaty hands can leave marks where moisture can settle, so it is a good idea to wipe tools down frequently with a lightly oiled cloth to prevent any rust forming.

GENERAL TOOLS

A selection of general woodworking tools will be needed, including:

- block plane and bench planes
- spokeshave
- cabinet scrapers
- a fine backsaw and a coping or fretsaw
- good-quality chisels and a gouge or two
- an accurate steel rule – either metric or imperial, but stick consistently to one or the other
- vernier or dial callipers
- an accurate try square or engineer's square
- some fine files and rasps
- a handheld drill (if you do not have a pillar drill) with Forstner and spur-point bits
- a selection of clamps, including some deep-throated ones.

An electric router is very useful. There is a miniature router base on the market which can be attached to a Dremel tool or similar, and this is invaluable for fine work such as cutting channels for purfling. A full-size router is the best tool for making the truss-rod channel.

Good-quality steel rules and dial or vernier callipers are essential. The all-metal engineer's square is likely to be more accurate than the traditional type with wooden stock

A good-quality smoothing plane (at rear) and a low-angle block plane. The miniature hand router (bottom left) is useful for cleaning out grooves and recesses

> ### TIP
>
> The following items will come in useful on many occasions:
>
> - 2in (50mm) plastic packing tape
> - small pieces of strong polythene tarpaulin sheet
> - small squares cut from translucent plastic food-storage boxes
> - bamboo chopsticks, various sizes
> - sanding sticks in various grits and widths, made by gluing abrasive paper to offcuts of hardwood
> - old bits of hacksaw blades
> - lead weights; you can mould these yourself in any convenient container.

Home-made sanding sticks; the one on the left has built-in fences to guide it

Cabinet scrapers are one of the luthier's favourite tools. Curved ones can either be bought or filed to shape from ordinary rectangular scrapers

STEP-BY-STEP GUITAR MAKING

SPECIALIST TOOLS

Here are some of the more specialized tools which it will be necessary or desirable to have:

- violin-makers' planes, for trimming linings and braces, and working in places inaccessible to ordinary planes
- thicknessing callipers, to monitor the thickness of soundboard and back
- bending iron, for bending ribs, purfling and linings
- purfling cutter, for marking and cutting the rebates for purfling and bindings
- slotting files, for cutting the string slots in the nut
- fretting hammer: this has a broad, smooth face; a jeweller's large-face hammer would be suitable

- a tapered reamer, for making the holes for the bridge pins
- a luthier's knife with a long, skewed point
- a purpose-made gauge for measuring the side-to-side curvature of the fretboard.

For bending the ribs, linings, purfling and bindings, a source of heat will be required. I use a proprietary mains electric bending iron. Other possibilities worth considering include:

- A steel box 4in (100mm) square with a hole in one side and a 3in (75mm) steel pipe welded to the top. Wood shavings and scraps are placed inside the box and lit. The pipe acts as a chimney, and when hot the chimney becomes the bending surface.

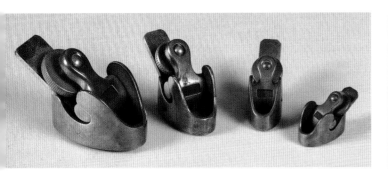

ABOVE LEFT The miniature planes intended for violin making are equally useful to the guitar maker

ABOVE A selection of small cutting tools; second from top is the traditional luthier's knife

FAR LEFT A smooth-faced hammer will be needed to install the frets

LEFT The bending iron. This commercial model is thermostatically controlled

BELOW LEFT A violin-maker's purfling cutter is used to score the rebates for purfling and binding

BELOW A reamer forms the tapered holes for the bridge pins

- A 3in (75mm) steel pipe, sealed at one end, held sideways in a machinist's vice, with a plumber's gas torch pointed into the pipe. The torch heats the pipe from inside, creating the hot bending surface.
- The **universal side-bending machine** can be purchased complete or made from plans. This device uses either 150-watt electric light bulbs or special electric blankets to provide the heat. You might want to consider this if you plan to build stringed instruments full-time.

When reducing the thickness of the soundboard, it is necessary to be able to reach into the middle of the plate and measure the thickness. You can invest in expensive dial-gauge callipers, or you can make your own from scraps of modellers' plywood, in which a wing nut is used to adjust the friction of the jaws, and the distance between the jaws is then measured using feeler gauges.

There are several methods of cutting out the circular channels for the soundhole inlay. I currently use a miniature router fitted with a purpose-made trammel base from a specialist supplier, but you can easily make a simple circle cutter from hardwood offcuts, as shown in the photo opposite.

MACHINERY

It is perfectly possible to build a fine guitar entirely by hand, but if you have some basic woodworking machines they will save you a lot of effort.

I have a bandsaw which will cut timber up to 8½in (215mm) thick if fed slowly. It is big enough to resaw material for backs and fronts, and for general day-to-day cutting. I have a 10in (255mm) tablesaw for general work, and a miniature one which has many uses. My woodturning lathe is used for turning items such as bridge pins, or small pins used for neck repairs. My pillar drill sees regular use. One other useful power tool that I have in my shop is a portable thickness planer which folds up and sits on a small trolley under a bench.

All my stationary power tools are connected to a permanently mounted dust-extraction system.

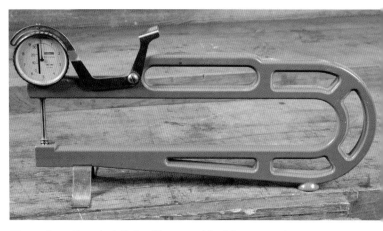

These deep-throated dial callipers are ideal for measuring soundboard thicknesses

A home-made circle cutter

A miniature tablesaw. This model is no longer made, but I believe there is now another one on the market

STEP-BY-STEP GUITAR MAKING

CLAMPING AND WORKHOLDING

Most of the preliminary work on the soundboard is done on a workboard, which is made from a piece of plywood, 20 x 24 x ¾in (510 x 610 x 18mm). A 1 x 2in (25 x 50mm) batten is attached to the underside of the plywood, 3in (75mm) in from one edge. A smaller batten, ¾in (18mm) square, is attached to one side of the larger batten, and another ¾in (18mm) square batten 3in (75mm) in from the opposite edge of the plywood. The larger batten is gripped in the main bench vice, while the two smaller battens keep the workboard up off the bench top to allow the soundboard to be clamped to it. A strip of wide plastic packing tape down the middle of the workboard protects the soundboard from being inadvertently glued to it.

The workboard installed in the bench vice

The assembly of the guitar takes place on the **solera**, which is described on pages 42–5.

For holding the guitar body when it is time for carving the neck or attaching the bridge, I use another plywood board, 1in (25mm) wider than the guitar body. Underneath is a 1 x 2in (25 x 50mm) batten with a 1in (25mm) square batten each side to allow the assembly to be held in my high-level vice (see below) with room for clamps underneath. Around its perimeter are wooden dowels 2½in (65mm) long by ⁵⁄₁₆in (8mm) diameter. A piece of smooth carpet or cloth is placed between the guitar body and the board, and the guitar is held firmly on the board by strong elastic straps hooked around the dowels. The straps are cut from scraps of sheet-rubber garden pond liner.

When shaping small components, I like to have them at a high level so I can work comfortably standing up. To do this I attached a small woodworking vice to an old oak drawer front, so the whole assembly can be mounted in the main bench vice. A small beech work surface is fitted behind the vice. You will see this high-level vice in use in many of the photographs; it is extremely useful for holding the guitar body by the neck when fitting the purfling and bindings, or for working on the fretboard, bridge and other components.

The high-level vice can be mounted in the bench vice in two different ways

LEFT The underside of the workboard, showing the layout of the battens

This workboard, shown mounted on the high-level vice, has dowels round the edge to secure rubber straps

To hold the soundboard bracing in place while the glue sets, I use a go-bar frame. This can be made from two pieces of ¾ or 1in (18 or 25mm) plywood separated by plywood corner plates; in my case, the underside of a high shelf acts as the top plate, and the workbench forms the lower plate. The distance between the top and bottom plates should be just enough for you to work comfortably between them. The go-bars are made from strips of resilient ash, ½ x ⅜in (13 x 10mm) and just slightly longer than the distance between the top of the brace and the underside of the top plate, so that they can be sprung firmly into position. I have several colour-coded sets of go-bars in different lengths to accommodate different heights of braces.

For clamping the linings to the ribs prior to fitting the rib assembly to the soundboard, I use plastic-faced metal spring clamps which I buy from a large DIY store when I visit the USA. For a cheaper alternative you can use large wooden clothes pegs (clothespins) with some rubber bands added for additional clamping pressure. This is a traditional method employed by violin makers and some Spanish guitar builders.

Commercial clamps are available for attaching the bridge to the soundboard. They can be expensive when you look at the accumulated price of three. Prior to investing in commercial clamps I made my own from strips of oak ¾in (19mm) square. The oak frame is not as rigid as a metal frame; this can be considered an advantage, as you cannot overtighten the clamp.

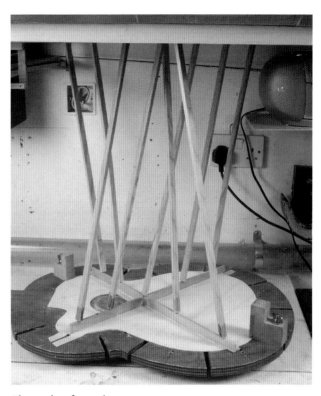

The go-bar frame in use

My collection of spring clamps

19

THE WORKSHOP

A general view of my workshop from the door, showing the main bench by the window, tool racks, lathe, pillar drill and secondary workbench with go-bar frame

Because the guitar is a relatively small item to construct, you do not require a large workshop. In fact, some builders of great repute have been known to build their guitars on the kitchen table, clearing it away at meal times. Others work in the attic or in a converted garage. My workshop is a small wooden shed, but well equipped and carefully planned.

Good light without shadows is essential, and natural daylight is best, so it is recommended that the work area be in front of a south-facing window if possible. I have fluorescent strip lights and low-voltage spotlights installed directly above my workbench; the spotlights have to be positioned and angled correctly so they won't blind you or overheat the area where you are working. All the windows in my workshop are double-glazed, and all of them open. I also have two non-opening, double-glazed roof

Halogen spotlights supplement the natural light

lights above and behind me, to let in the early morning light. You can never have too much light in your workshop. When the weather is hot I open the windows and turn on my ceiling-mounted fan to circulate the air. My bandsaw run-out area faces a large opening window, so when I have long pieces of wood to rip I merely open the window and push the wood through.

The window behind the bandsaw can be opened to accommodate long pieces

You might consider renting or leasing a commercial workshop, which would give you plenty of building space and can be a joy to work in, but you will need to bear in mind the cost of the rent, taxes, security, commercial insurance, heating and lighting. If you plan to build guitars for a living, you will need to factor all these costs into the final price of your instruments and still be competitive. Your workshop will display a professional appearance to your customers, but may also attract the attention of local officials, ever eager to inspect your safety equipment, fire prevention, dust extraction and waste disposal methods.

A garden shed is wonderful in the summer, with the door and window open to the gentle summer breezes; the same shed in winter can be like an ice cave in Alaska. A constant temperature will help in maintaining a constant humidity level, which is important for the stability of the instruments you make and the wood you have in storage. I have a small, oil-filled electric heater in my 9 x 12ft (2.7 x 3.6m) workshop; it is equipped with a thermostat to maintain a comfortable working temperature.

Having a small workshop means that I have to be inventive when it comes to using space. All the hand tools I use are held in wooden racks just in front of, beside and above my work area, so I never have to fumble in a drawer, where tools may roll around and become blunted. My planes, spokeshaves and measuring devices each have their own individual storage space. I group my hand tools according to their uses, so as to be able to locate just the item I need when I need it.

Tool racks surround the main working area

BELOW LEFT Planes and other small tools are housed to the right of the workbench

BELOW Chisels, saws, spokeshaves and metalworking tools occupy racks at one end of the main bench

BOTTOM The roof space is not wasted: overhead storage accommodates plans and purfling strips

Ducting connects all the power tools to my extraction unit

All my workshop power tools are connected to a plumbed-in dust-extraction system. These systems can be purchased from the larger tool distributors and quality tool shops, and they are very effective – on the odd occasion when the hose gets clogged I am inundated by a fine film of dust requiring much effort in cleaning up. If you plan to build with virtually no power tools, then the dust and shavings created are relatively easy to contain.

I have a secondary workbench that I use when I am waiting for glue to dry and I want to keep the main workbench clear for other work; my go-bar frame (see page 19) is located here. A third, smaller bench is equipped with a metalworking vice and a small bench grinder. I find this extra vice very useful to hold small jigs.

TOP Prepared timber and a portable tablesaw nestle beneath the second workbench; the bending mould and high-level vice can be seen in the foreground

ABOVE The bench grinder and metalworking vice

There are two devices that create noise in my workshop. The first is the combination of bandsaw and dust extractor – although when running together they are not any noisier than a vacuum cleaner. The only exception is when the bandsaw blade becomes dull; in this condition it is useless for accurate cutting and is also unsafe to use, so it must be changed for a sharp one. The other noisy tool is the thickness planer, which I seldom use; when I do, I wear ear defenders.

A bundle of guitar ribs, securely packed with stickers between

Timber for future guitars is stickered – that is, stacked with small spacers between to allow the air to circulate – and tightly held between sheets of ¾in (18mm) plywood bound with tape. The bundles are stored under one of the workbenches, out of harm's way.

I am fortunate to have space for a spray booth, and a separate area for setting up and adjusting guitars, away from the dust and (carefully organized) clutter of the main workshop.

Security in the workshop is very important. As your skills increase you will probably find guitar owners asking you to do repairs or adjustments, and you owe it to your customers and your own peace of mind to provide the best security that you can. Fitting alarms to the doors and windows is a good idea. Hinged solid shutters with drop bars to the inside are also useful. Some insurance companies offer specific policies for craft workers that will cover your workshop, tools and instruments under construction. Get a good-quality fire extinguisher and have it tested regularly.

PROTECTING THE ENVIRONMENT

Building guitars is a very organic occupation for me, and does not in itself produce hazardous waste. I separate any usable wood scraps and give them to an acquaintance who makes miniature musical instruments. Clean paper goes to the recycling centre. The sawdust and shavings go on the garden paths for a weed-mulch, and the very small remainder of waste – sandpaper, old glue brushes, etc. – goes into the regular rubbish collection about once a month. I am always looking for ways to recycle.

ABOVE My spray booth

BELOW This area is used for setting up and minor repairs

HEALTH AND SAFETY

I dislike wearing gloves, but when working this close to a hot bending iron they are definitely recommended

Before starting on the construction of our guitar, a word on safety. Safety procedures exist for your protection and must never be ignored. This book deals with the process of hand-building a guitar, so the advice given here relates to work performed mostly by hand in a small workshop.

- Never work when you are tired, taking medication that may make you drowsy, or under the influence of alcohol. Making musical instruments requires the full use of your faculties.
- All cutting tools need to be kept super-sharp, so they must always be treated with great respect. Paradoxically, dull tools can be more dangerous, because they require more pressure and may behave unpredictably.
- If you are unsure about setting up or using any of the tools or machinery you have bought, talk to your supplier. Many reputable suppliers run classes on the products they sell. If they are not able to help, look up your local adult education classes.
- Electrical equipment and the associated cables need to be inspected regularly, with a thorough going-over at least once a year. Check cables for loose parts, fraying or split outer covers. Make sure the plug is wired with the correct polarity – a tool with the plug wired in reverse is still live when switched off. Is the fuse, if fitted, the correct rating for the tool? Is all the machinery properly earthed? If in doubt, have your electrical equipment inspected once a year by a certified electrician who can issue an industry-approved certificate. Some insurance companies now require such a certificate; your workshop is insured, isn't it?
- A lot of heat is involved in the rib-bending process, and it is a good idea to wear insulating gloves. Some woods, such as cocobolo (*Dalbergia retusa*), give off a lot of steam and gas when being bent, and it is advisable to wear a breathing mask rated for organic vapours.

- Wood shavings and sawdust left on the floor constitute a fire hazard. Smoking in a workshop should never be tolerated: a carelessly discarded cigarette, pipe or cigar could easily burn down the whole workshop and other structures nearby.

- Jewellery should not be worn, and that includes watches, necklaces, etc., which can become trapped in machinery. If you have swollen knuckles and are unable to remove your wedding ring, at least tape it up with sticking plaster so that nothing can catch under the band. Avoid loose clothing, and if you hair is long, tie it back out of the way.

- Always wear a dust mask when sanding or using power tools. *All* dust is harmful, but dust from certain hardwoods, in particular, can cause breathing problems – and the dangers are not limited to exotic species. All power tools should be connected to a dust-extraction system, as described on page 22.

- Modern shellac polishes, as used in French polishing, include industrial alcohol solvents, and need to be treated with the same care as solvent-based lacquers. Goggles or a full-face mask should be worn when spraying solvent-based finishes (there is more advice about this in the panel opposite). Overexposure to the gases given off during the drying stages of solvent-based finishes can cause permanent nerve damage.

The safety advice in this book is provided for your guidance, but cannot cover all eventualities; the safe use of hand and power tools is ultimately the responsibility of the user. If you are unhappy about a particular procedure, don't use it – there is always another way.

WARNING

SAFETY PRECAUTIONS WHEN SPRAYING LACQUER

1 Always work in a well-ventilated, tidy, dust-free, dry and well-lit area.
2 Never smoke or have open flames in or near the work area.
3 Always wear a suitable respirator, preferably one that protects the eyes from overspray; it must be a model that is rated for organic fumes.
4 Wear a suitable apron or overalls to protect skin and clothing.
5 Do not spray in the house, or where children and animals may breathe the fumes.

Avoid overexposure to the gases given off during the drying stages of lacquer.

If you keep your safety gear near where you need to use it, you are less likely to be tempted to manage without. This safety visor hangs ready near my pillar drill, which is used for drum sanding

BUILDING METHODS

There are basically three methods of making a guitar body, all of which work well and will produce a very fine instrument.

1 The first method is one traditionally employed in the construction of violins. An internal mould is cut from plywood or hardwood to the inside body shape of the instrument. The ribs are temporarily clamped to the mould after bending, and are then glued to the end and heel blocks and the whole assembly held in the mould till the glue has set. A modified violin mould laminated from thicker sections of plywood can be used to make guitar bodies. This method works well, but limits the guitar shape to that of the mould. One advantage is that a bending former need not be made, as the body mould itself will suffice.

2 The second method is the reverse of the first, using an outside mould with a cut-out in the shape of the guitar, into which the ribs are bent and clamped. Once again, a bending former is not needed. This method also limits the body shape to that of the mould.

3 If you plan to build guitars of different shapes and hand-bend the ribs, then the **solera** method described in the text is the most efficient. It allows you to change the body shape without making new moulds; all that is necessary is to draw a different shape on the board and set the clamping blocks to the new outline. However, if you plan to make more than one guitar of a given shape, it will be useful to make a half-body-shaped mould as described below, in addition to the solera.

The outside mould is made in two halves, and the lugs at the ends serve to secure these together

A guitar taking shape on the solera

Interchangeable blocks enable the same bending mould to be used both for the standard-shape rib on the bass side of the guitar ...

... and the cutaway rib on the treble side. Does it remind you of a pig?

A bending mould – sometimes referred to as a 'pig' because of its shape – allows any number of ribs to be bent to a consistent outline. In the version shown here, the blocks at the front of the mould are interchangeable to make either a standard-shape

body or a cutaway body, which can be either right- or left-handed. Holes are cut to facilitate the use of clamps and cauls to hold the rib in place while cooling and setting takes place. This type of mould can be used in a rib-bending machine, like the interchangeable dies in an engineering press.

For the standard acoustic guitar I prefer to use the solera and male bending mould. This is the method illustrated in this book.

There are two ways of assembling the guitar:
• Build the body first, then attach the neck to it, as on a violin.
• Make the neck first, then assemble the body around it. This is the traditional Spanish method, and is the procedure followed in this book. It makes for a more rigid instrument, less likely to distort under string tension.

In the Spanish system of construction, the root of the neck is the core around which the body of the guitar is assembled

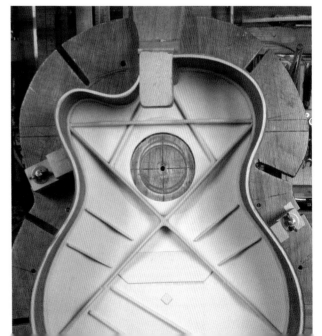

SCHEDULE OF OPERATIONS

To help you orientate yourself during the building process, here is a summary of the various stages as they are described in the book.

Preparation

Select timber (pages 30–5) and mark out
Make workboard, solera, moulds and templates (18–19, 42–5)

Neck and endblock

Prepare neck timber (46–8)
Assemble neck blocks and head plate (48–50)
Clean all surfaces on neck blank (50)
Mark out neck for truss rod (51)
Install truss rod (51–2)
Cut out heel shape on neck, and seal (52–4)
Make and fit head veneers (54–6)
Mark out head details (55)
Cut head shape and drill holes for machine tuners (56)
Cut endblock to size, shape, sand and seal (57)

Soundboard

Prepare soundboard plates, joint and glue plates together (58–9)

Clean soundboard glue lines and mark guitar outline on board (60)
Make and fit soundhole decoration (61–5)
Cut out shape of soundboard, tune to thickness and mark brace positions (66–7)
Make and fit soundhole backing plate (68–9)
Cut out soundhole (69)
Make main X-brace and shape to fit soundboard on solera (70–2)
Glue braces to soundboard (73–5)
Shape and sand braces (73–5)

Ribs

Prepare ribs and bend to shape (76–81)
Prepare, bend and attach front linings to ribs (82–3)

Back

Prepare back plates, joint and glue plates together (84–6)
Clean glue lines and mark guitar outline on board (86–7)
Glue and shape back-seam stiffening strip (87)
Cut out shape of back, reduce to final thickness and mark brace positions (87)
Cut back braces, fit and glue to back (88–9)

Assembly

Dry-fit neck and endblock (90–2)

Dry-fit ribs to soundboard and prepare ends to fit into rib slots on neck (91)

Glue neck and endblock to soundboard (92–3)

Glue ribs to soundboard assembly (93–5)

Shape back contact surfaces of ribs and attach back linings (95–6)

Fit and glue back to guitar body (97–9)

Purfling and bindings

Make purfling and binding strips (100–1)

Make and fit end-seam inlay (101–2)

Rout rebates in body (102–4)

Fit purfling and bindings to back of guitar, then to soundboard (104–6)

Fit head bindings if required (107)

Fretboard

Prepare timber (108–9)

Mark out and cut fret slots (109–10)

Taper sides of fretboard (110)

Fit bindings to fretboard if required (111)

Radius fretboard surface and true end to end (112)

Fit and glue fretboard to neck (113–14)

Fit fret-position markers (115)

Fit frets (116–18)

Dress frets (118–19)

Final shaping of neck and head

Remove surplus timber from neck (120–1)

Radius neck and blend into heel and head (121)

Bridge

Make the bridge (122–5)

Prepare bridge to fit soundboard (125)

Mark out bridge position (126–7)

Finishing

Prepare working area (128–9)

Prepare surfaces (129–31)

Stain if required (131)

Fill grain (132–3)

Apply finish (132–3)

Polish (133)

Final stages

Attach bridge and saddle (134–7)

Make and fit top nut (137)

Fit tuners (138)

Attach strings (138)

Set action of strings (138–9)

Tune the guitar (139)

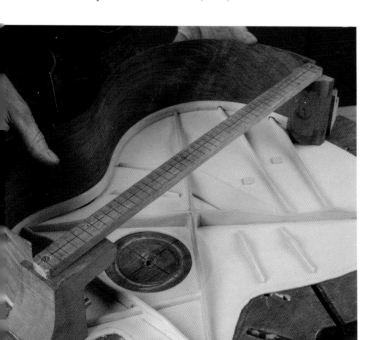
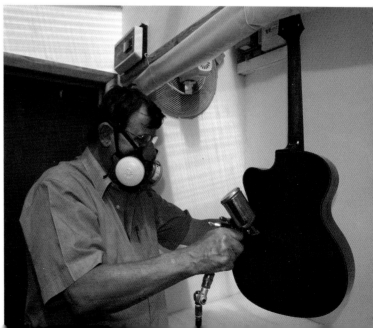

WOOD SELECTION

A highly figured piece of Brazilian rosewood (*Dalbergia nigra*) recovered from a tree stump

Selecting your material is the first step in making a guitar, and in some ways the most important. By all means choose plain wood for your first instruments – it is less expensive and easier to work than highly figured wood – but don't be tempted to skimp on the quality, or your efforts will come to nothing.

If you are buying from a specialist luthier supplier, most of the work of preparing the timber to rough shape will have been done by them. For most of us this is the best way to purchase timber. Your local builders' centre may have spruce and what they call mahogany, but it will not necessary be the same species, or be of good enough quality for making fine guitars. (A rare exception is the very fine guitar made by the American firm Taylor Guitars from a wooden pallet recycled in their workshop.)

It is possible to purchase complete guitar kits from luthier suppliers, though this limits you to the woods and parts that they have picked off their storage racks. If this is to be your first guitar, then this can be an excellent way of keeping the cost down; the supplier provides everything you need in one package, and the sides may be already bent to shape, which is a great saving in time and money if you consider the cost of a bending iron.

If you decide to select your own timber, the following pages provide some guidance. Please note that this list is not exhaustive, and that not all the woods that are listed will be available from all luthier suppliers at any given time. Tracking down the materials you require is part of the excitement of instrument making.

WOOD AND THE ENVIRONMENT

Much has been written recently about renewable resources, and how the lungs of the world, the forests, are being destroyed by overdevelopment. This fact has led to certain timber species, such as

Brazilian or Rio rosewood (*Dalbergia nigra*), being virtually unobtainable. However, there are still some suppliers who can offer legally sourced Brazilian rosewood, and provide a passport of authentication to show that the timber is approved by CITES (the Convention on International Trade in Endangered Species of Wild Flora and Fauna). Another approved source of this timber is recycled rosewood tree stumps, reclaimed from trees felled more than half a century ago; the rosewood used for the guitar shown in this book was sourced in this way.

Deforestation would not be such a problem if trees that are cut were replaced with new saplings, thus maintaining a sustainable supply; but much of the tree cutting in Brazil, for example, is done to create grazing ground for beef cattle to feed the ever-growing Western appetite for fast food.

One tree in a forest will consume an average of 20lb (9kg) of carbon dioxide in a year, with an acre (0.4 hectare) consuming on average five tons (5.1 tonnes) per year. For every ton and a half of carbon dioxide absorbed by the trees, one ton of oxygen is released into the atmosphere. It is interesting to note that old-growth forest trees consume less carbon dioxide than a similar acreage of young trees, so it is actually beneficial to recycle the forest, planting new trees as you fell the old ones.

WHAT TO LOOK FOR

Logs are cut in a variety of configurations, of which the most important are flatsawing and quarter-sawing. **Flatsawn** wood, typical of most cut timber in builders' supply depots, is obtained by running the tree trunk back and forward through the saw, making parallel cuts as in sliced bread. This is an economical method, but the wood is not very stable – that is, it is liable to warp with variations in humidity. **Quartersawn** timber is cut more or less radially, like segments of an orange, so that its grain runs at right angles to the surface of the finished piece. There is more wastage with this method, but

the wood is stable, and many species produce particularly attractive figure when cut in this way. (**Figure** refers to the patterns produced on the surface of wood by the configuration of the grain and other natural features.)

Flat or plain sawing produces little wastage, but the lie of the grain in the resulting boards encourages warping

Though quartersawn timber is less economical, it makes more stable boards. The best boards are those from the centre of each wedge

Sitka spruce (*Picea sitchensis*)

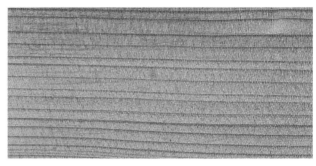

European spruce (*Picea abies*)

Guitar **tops** or **soundboards** are usually made from quartersawn softwood such as spruce (various *Picea* species), western red cedar (*Thuja plicata*), or sometimes American redwood (*Sequoia sempervirens*). The functional characteristics of these timbers are similar, although their colour and density are different. The optimum final thickness will also differ: typically about ⁵⁄₆₄in (2mm) for spruce tops and ⅛in (3mm) for cedar, with redwood somewhere in between. The most commonly used wood for guitar tops is Sitka spruce (*Picea sitchensis*), one of the seven spruce species available. Cedar and redwood give a very bright, immediate sound, popular in Flamenco music and also with fingerstylists, while spruce takes time to mature, finally giving a complexity of sound much loved by classical musicians, jazz guitarists and certain fingerstyle players.

Before you start building, have a look at the soundboard timber. Seen from the end, it should display a grain pattern that is as close to vertical as possible. The two halves of the soundboard should be **bookmatched**; this means that a single piece of wood has been cut in half through its thickness so that when the two leaves are opened like the pages of a book, one is a mirror image of the other. Lay the two pieces side by side on the workbench in good light and look at the grain. Do they match as if one side was being looked at in a mirror? Move them around till the grain of one mirrors the other. Look for grain runout on the edges where the plates meet: ideally the grain in each plate edge should be

SITKA FACTS

Early on in the aircraft industry, Sitka spruce was the chosen material for airframes and wings; and it is still the choice wood for aeroplane kit makers and restorers. Its popularity is due to its lightness, strength and availability. It grows mostly in the Pacific coast region of North America, from southern Alaska down to north-west California. The biggest specimen ever recorded stood 216ft (66m) high with a diameter of 16.7ft (5.1m). Aircraft specification requires vertical grain with at least six annual rings per inch (25mm), with minimum grain runout. The requirements for guitar tops are more stringent: at least double that amount is preferable, with some top grades having as many as 45 rings per inch.

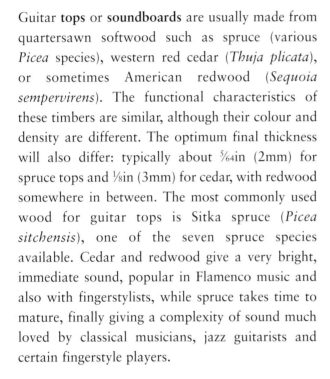

Bookmatched spruce for a guitar soundboard

Macassar ebony (*Diospyros celebica*)

Ziricote (*Cordia dodecandra*)

parallel, and not run off the edge of the board at an angle. A slight runout can be accepted where the grain is not perfectly parallel. If the grain is straight and there is noticeable runout, then the plate edges will need to be planed to provide parallel grain.

Decide which side you want to be the outside face of the soundboard. It is a good idea at this time to mark the inside faces at the neck end; I use a soft white wax pencil for this. Next, lay the body template on top of the wood and decide where on the wood you want to cut the top from; take a soft black pencil and mark around the outline. This helps with orientation when it comes to planing the edges prior to gluing the top plates together. When you get them from the supplier, they will have been cut to between ³⁄₁₆ and ¹⁄₄in thick (4–6mm), leaving plenty of room to plane the surface after gluing.

The **bracing** on the inside of the soundboard is usually made from vertical-grained Sitka spruce, while the back bracing can be made from spruce, maple (*Acer* sp.) or African mahogany (*Khaya* sp.).

Linings are the narrow strips of timber that provide for a wider gluing surface between sides and back, and between sides and soundboard. Traditionally these would be made from single pieces of timber, steam-bent and glued to the rib prior to its being fitted to the soundboard. Fine Spanish classical guitars often use strips of kerfed timber instead, and a third alternative is to use individual blocks, glued in one at a time.

The **back** and **sides** of the guitar are usually made from a decorative hardwood. This was traditionally Brazilian rosewood, but now that it

has become scarce other equally beautiful woods are being used, such as Madagascar rosewood (*Dalbergia baronii* and related species), Macassar ebony (*Diospyros celebica*) or ziricote (*Cordia dodecandra*), to mention only three of the 20-odd species that are suitable for top-quality guitars. Backs and sides, like soundboards, are normally bookmatched.

A bookmatched guitar back in Brazilian rosewood (*Dalbergia nigra*)...

...and a matching pair of ribs

33

African mahogany (*Khaya ivorensis*)

African ebony (*Diospyros crassiflora*)

Hard or rock maple (*Acer saccharum*)

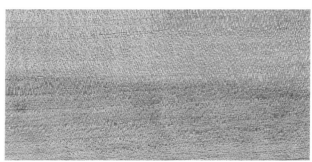

European sycamore (*Acer pseudoplatanus*), actually a maple species despite its name

On a fretless instrument, such as the violin family or some bass guitars, the strings are stopped on a smooth fingerboard; the equivalent part on a fretted instrument is usually called the **fretboard**. Timbers typically used for fretboards are ebony, rosewood and maple (*Diospyros, Dalbergia, Acer* spp.). Maple, being light in colour, needs to be sealed, or it will turn black with exposure to sweat and finger oils. Some guitar makers are using coloured superglue for this purpose, in place of the traditional lacquer finish. **Bridges** can be made from most of the timbers used for the back and sides, although the usual choice is rosewood or ebony.

Acoustic guitar **necks** need to be light and strong. The principal choice is easily worked Brazilian mahogany (*Swietenia macrophylla* or *S. mahagoni*). The grain, although highly interlocked, cuts, sands, glues and stains well, and the wood is very stable.

A second-choice timber would be Spanish cedar (*Cedrela odorata*), which, despite its name, originates from Brazil and other South and Central American countries. It is similar to Brazilian mahogany, except that the grain is more interlocking and can tear out when being worked.

Toona (*Toona ciliata*) has the general appearance of mahogany, but with a more open pore structure. It works extremely well, and is light. The colour of the wood is red, with a pink hue; it is sometimes called Australian red cedar.

Other timbers can be used, such as sycamore and flamed maple, as seen on the necks of fine violins and modern electric guitars.

For a stiffer or more colourful neck, or if timber is scarce, a laminated construction using three pieces of timber can be adopted. An advantage of building a laminated neck is that the centre section can be made the same width as the truss rod, saving the work of routing a truss-rod groove. Using maple for the outside sections and padauk (*Pterocarpus* sp.) for the centre section will give the neck an interesting look. Even birch plywood has sometimes been used, but there is no guarantee that it will be strong enough.

Brazilian mahogany (*Swietenia macrophylla*)

Toona or Australian red cedar (*Toona ciliata*)

Andaman padauk (*Pterocarpus dalbergioides*)

African padauk (*Pterocarpus soyauxii*)

The timbers discussed on the previous pages are the more common ones available for the making of musical instruments. Suppliers who specialize in tonewoods may well have a more extensive range, and their catalogues often contain much valuable information. Sometimes a call to one of these suppliers will turn up an interesting species which they have not included in their catalogue – perhaps because it is only seasonally available in small quantities. It is best to stick to the more familiar and readily available species for your first instruments, but once you have some experience you may wish to explore more widely.

English yew (*Taxus baccata*) is a striking and unusual choice for the back of this guitar, known as the Rose of Heligan. The whole instrument is made from woods sourced from the Lost Gardens of Heligan, a great Victorian garden in Cornwall, England, that was recently restored and opened to the public

A glue pot for use with hide glue. This modern electric model is thermostatically controlled, and a warning light reminds you when it is on

A steel-string guitar is made from approximately 129 pieces of wood, and a classical guitar has even more. They are held together almost entirely by glue, so the fitting of parts must be precise and the choice of glues is very important.

A notable ocean sailor, in an account of his single-handed round-the-world voyage, recalls how he would lie in his bunk during a storm thinking of all the nails that he had bent over, instead of pulling them out and replacing them. In guitar making we do not have the luxury of using metal fasteners, even bent ones – the only fasteners in a guitar are the small screws that hold the machine tuners in position to stop them rotating under string tension, and, if fitted, the strap button.

Because stringed instruments inevitably need repairing sooner or later, it is preferable to use glues that can be undone when necessary. I always try to think of my guitars, possibly 50 years or more from now, being serviced in a workshop; the luthier should have a comparatively easy job because I have used traditional glues, finishes and techniques in their construction. The magnificent violins made by Amati, Guarneri and Stradivari rely only on hide glue and varnish, commingled with a love of what they were creating.

The luthier has a wide choice of glues to use, ranging from the aerospace industry's superglue (cyanoacrylate) down to the well-tried animal glues which have been in use for centuries. Each type has its advantages in different situations.

Hide glue – sometimes referred to as **animal glue** or **pearl glue** – is made from the boiled-down bones and hides of animals, and is excellent for structural gluing and for repairs to older instruments. It cleans up with warm water and a cloth. Its fast initial 'grab' allows you to place a patch inside the body of a guitar, press it into place and leave it without clamping; as the glue cools and sets, it shrinks, pulling the patch tighter. The glue granules are mixed with water, then heated – not boiled – in a double boiler. The glue is applied hot, and sets by cooling and evaporation. It can be reheated within reason, and new glue can even be added over old. It is used extensively in violin making and repairs, as it is a relatively simple job to take an instrument apart without damage. Wherever these unique properties are required, hide glue is the best there is.

Polyvinyl acetate (PVA) glues are the most prevalent types in woodwork today, available in most DIY stores. They are supplied pre-mixed, ready to use, and can be cleaned up with water. There are three main types:

• **White PVA** is not suitable for instrument making, as it sets soft, so the joint can creep under tension. It is difficult to sand, and if spills are not cleaned up promptly it will stain the wood; sometimes this is not apparent till the finish is applied.

• **Yellow glue**, sometimes known as **aliphatic resin glue**, is an improvement on the white, as it contains more solids, making it hard when set and thus easier to sand. It sets more quickly, but has a shorter open time, which means that there is less opportunity to reposition the components once they have been pressed together.

• **Cross-linking PVA glue** is probably the best all-round glue available. It too is yellow, but it is more water-resistant than the previous types of yellow glue. The colour when set is dark amber, making it quite suitable for guitar making. It is available in containers as small as 8 fl oz (230ml), up to industrial-sized barrels. It has a long shelf life in the container, cleans up readily with water, and sets quickly.

Urea-formaldehyde and resorcinol glues are excellent for structural joints such as laminated beams. They are supplied in the form of a powdered catalyst and a liquid resin. Note that the fumes given off during curing can cause an allergic reaction in some people.

Epoxy resin is an industrial glue used mainly on difficult materials such as oily hardwoods, which are resistant to other glues. It is also used to repair structures that will be subject to heavy loading, such as broken necks on guitars. It is normally available only through wholesale outlets, although small consumer-sized tubes are available from DIY stores.

Epoxy resins are supplied as two separate components which must be mixed together immediately before use

Epoxy has good gap-filling abilities, especially when mixed with thixotropic additives, and can be thinned for better penetration into the timber.

I use **cyanoacrylate** or **superglue** for inlaying shell material and repairing stress cracks in parts such as fretboards or bridges. It is excellent for filling holes in dark woods, when mixed with similar-coloured wood dust.

For most purposes I use the traditional animal glue, with the remaining joints being glued with yellow aliphatic glue.

FITTINGS AND ACCESSORIES

There are no nails, screws or bolts in a guitar, except for the locking screws in machine tuners and, if fitted, the screw for a strap button. There are certain accessories, though, without which the guitar would not function.

TRUSS RODS

Built into most guitar necks is the truss rod, whose purpose is to hold the neck flat and straight against the tension of the strings. The necks of the older gut- and nylon-strung guitars were stiffened with a piece of hardwood, such as ebony. Early steel-strung guitars used a flat strip of mild steel, which over time developed into a rod with a threaded section at one end, permitting adjustment for various tensions caused by different string gauges. Most truss rods are adjusted from inside the body of the guitar. Mandolins, on the other hand, use a curved rod set into a curved groove in the neck, with a threaded,

adjustable section at the head end, usually hidden under a decorative plate fixed with two to three small screws.

Some makers, striving for a light and stiff neck, set in strips of carbon fibre. This high-tech material allows for a very small cross-section in the neck, and, when combined with an adjustable truss rod, will give a very stable neck. This method is especially good for long necks, as on baritone and bass guitars.

MACHINE TUNERS

For a stringed instrument to play properly in tune, the strings need to have their tension adjusted and then reliably held. Tapered friction pegs are still the norm on instruments such as violins and cellos, but with the advent of high-tension steel strings on guitars, a more secure method was called for.

The method used today is the geared machine tuner, available in 15 : 1 or 18 : 1 gear ratios, which gives a very accurate and smooth adjustment to the string tension. These can be in the form of a single unit with three tuners mounted on a decorative plate on each side of the head, as is seen in classical nylon-strung guitars. However, most modern steel-strung guitars use single machine tuners, fitted three on each side of the head, or even six on one side, as in

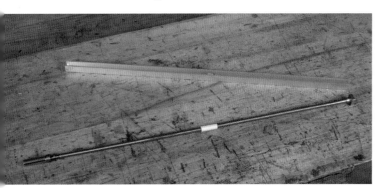

The truss rod, dismantled to show the screw mechanism and the outer casing

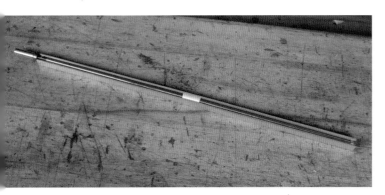

The truss rod fully assembled

A typical single tuner for a steel-string guitar

the classic Fender guitars. Machine tuners are available in a range of colours and finishes, including black, nickel, chrome and gold. There are even handmade tuners available from specialist makers in materials such as gold, silver, bronze and stainless steel. The buttons also come in various shapes, sizes and materials.

BRIDGE PINS

The other end of the string needs to be anchored securely. On classical nylon-strung guitars the strings are fastened to a tie-bar which is incorporated into the bridge. In the majority of steel-strung guitars, a small, tapered pin is pushed into a similarly tapered hole in the bridge, trapping the string. The string sits in a groove whose width corresponds to the diameter of the wound end of the string, while the ball end of the string is trapped against the bridge backing plate on the inside of the soundboard. The bridge pin is held in place by friction, trapping the string in the groove. The pin's job is not to hold the string under tension, but simply to trap it in position.

Bridge pins can be made from plastic, or lathe-turned from a decorative hardwood such as ebony or rosewood; they are usually decorated with an inlaid button of mother-of-pearl or abalone shell.

FRET WIRE

Frets are used to stop the string at predetermined positions on the fretboard, providing a clear note and reliable intonation. Early fretted instruments used loops of gut tied around the neck. The first metal frets were made from a rectangular-section brass strip. Modern fret wire is formed from 18% hard nickel-silver alloy, which is an amalgam of brass (copper and zinc) and nickel; it is the nickel which gives the wire its silver colour. The addition of nickel gives a long service life to the fret, even when guitars are strung with steel strings. Fret wire is available in many crown sizes and tang depths. The size of the crown (the part which is exposed above the fretboard surface) affects the playability of the guitar, while a deeper tang (the part fixed into the fretboard) will grip the slot better.

Tuners mounted in groups of three, for use on guitars with a slotted head

A set of bridge pins

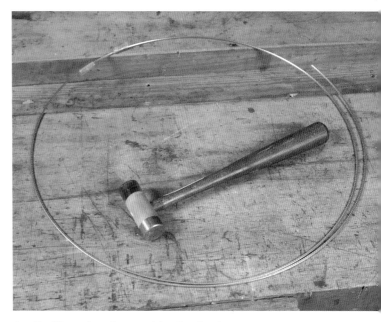

A coil of fret wire, shown with a fretting hammer

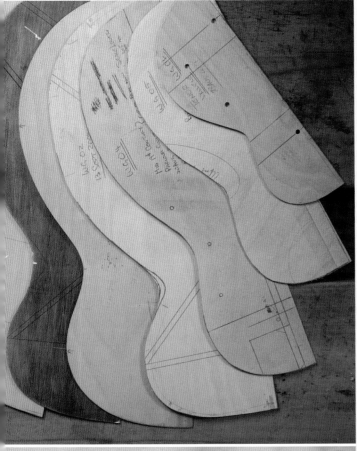

PART 2

GUITAR MAKING STEP BY STEP

1 THE TEMPLATE AND SOLERA

The half-template laid on the solera

Solera is a Spanish word meaning a sill or a foundation stone. In guitar making, the solera is the baseboard on which the body of the instrument is constructed. It is more versatile than a solid mould, because it can be adjusted to accommodate a range of different body shapes.

MAKING THE TEMPLATE

1 Tape some pieces of carbon paper together and lay them on the ⅛in (3mm) plywood with the ink face down. Lay the plan on top with about ½in (13mm) of the thin ply protruding beyond the centre line of the guitar. Carefully trace the half-outline of the guitar, including the centre line, using a fine ballpoint pen. Mark the soundhole centre; draw perpendicular lines across the widest part of the upper bout, the narrowest part of the waist and the widest part of the lower bout. If you are making a cutaway model, as shown on the enclosed full-size plans, draw the shape of the cutaway *as well as* the full outline. Remove the plan and the carbon paper, and check that you have a full half-outline of the body, complete with the centre line. Using a coping saw or similar, cut out the shape of the half-template and carefully sand down to the line. You may find it helpful to draw the positions of the internal braces for future reference.

MATERIALS

For the solera:
- ¾in (18mm) plywood, 24 x 36in (900 x 600mm)

For the template:
- ⅛in (3mm) plywood, 24 x 12in (600 x 300mm)

For clamps and cauls:
- 2in (50mm) hardwood dowel (or rolling pin) cut into 1½in (40mm) lengths
- Beech or other hardwood, 4 x 3 x 45in (100 x 75 x 1150mm)
- ⁵⁄₁₆in (M8) threaded steel rod (studding)
- ⁵⁄₁₆in (8mm) wing nuts
- ⁵⁄₁₆in (8mm) plate washers
- Thin cork sheet, e.g. offcuts from cork floor tiles

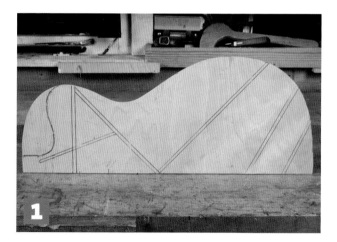

2 Rather than making a second template for the cutaway side, you can use a small drill bit and file to cut a series of slots along the line of the cutaway. When using the template, you draw through the slots and then join up the gaps by eye.

3 You may build up a large collection of templates during your guitar-making career. Label them carefully and keep them in a safe place.

MAKING THE SOLERA

4 I prefer to use soft mahogany construction-grade plywood for the solera, as it is easy to carve out the depression which receives the arching of the soundboard. Lay the ¾in (18mm) plywood flat on the bench and draw a centre line down the whole length of the board. Very accurately mark the position of the centre of the soundhole. Lay your template along the centre line of the board, with its lower end about 4in (100mm) from the edge of the plywood. Using a soft pencil, draw round the template to give the half-outline of the body. Reverse the template onto the other side of the centre line, making sure the soundhole position and both ends of the template are aligned as before, then draw the other side. You should now have the full outline of the guitar body on the plywood. The guitar will lie face down on the solera; remember this when drawing the shape of the cutaway.

To support the neck end of the guitar during construction, a neck extension needs to be incorporated into the solera. Extend the centre line out about 13in (330mm) from the neck end of the body outline, and draw lines parallel to the centre line, about 2in (50mm) either side of it; you should now have what looks like a stubby neck outline.

When you are sure that the shape of the body is fair, go over the pencil line with ballpoint pen, pressing hard to create an indented outline of the guitar body. At a suitable location, mark this line with the guitar model and the date. This will avoid confusion if you later re-use the solera for a different model.

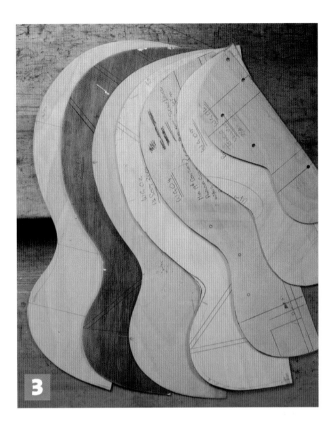

To allow for the slightly domed face of the guitar, use a violin-maker's plane to scoop out a ⅛in (3mm) depression in the face of the solera. As you cut through the veneers of the plywood you will be able to see a sort of contour map of the three-dimensional shape of the dome.

Draw a line about 4in (100mm) outside the outline of the guitar body and neck, and cut away the surplus to give the final shape of the solera.

5 The 11 slots for the clamping blocks extend from the perimeter of the solera to just outside the body outline. Start by drilling a hole at the inside end of each slot, just large enough to accommodate your threaded rod, then saw in towards the hole. The slots are spaced fairly evenly around the guitar outline, but may be placed closer together in the waist area, where the curve is tighter. Make the L-shaped rib-clamping blocks from any available hardwood. They are attached to the solera with coach bolts or with threaded rod, secured by a washer and wing nut at each end.

6 Small hardwood blocks are glued to the underside of the solera, just outside the guitar outline and equally spaced between the clamping slots. I used a 2in (50mm) diameter beechwood rolling pin, cut into 1½in (40mm) lengths. A tapping hole for a ⁵⁄₁₆in (M8) thread is drilled through the front of the solera into each of these blocks. These holes are for fitting the threaded rods for the spool clamps used to hold the ribs down during the assembly of the guitar. The blocks also

NECK ANGLE

Classical guitars have their necks angled slightly forward, whereas flat-top and arch-top instruments have theirs either flat or set back. For the flat-top guitar we are making, the surface of the solera should be left flat, with the neck extension in the same plane as the body section. For a classical guitar, you would need to plane a taper on the neck extension, starting at the neck-to-body joint and removing a thickness of about ⁵⁄₆₄in (2mm) at the far end of the neck support. You can accommodate both types on one solera by making a removable shim.

TIP

Line the spool clamps and the L-shaped blocks with cork on the surfaces that will come into contact with the guitar.

raise the solera off the bench so that clamps can fit underneath while gluing. Drill an additional hole for a spool clamp in the cutaway area.

7 I make two kinds of spool clamps, both using threaded rod, hardwood dowel, washers and wing nuts. Some have a length of dowel at the top only, the lower end being screwed into the threaded holes in the solera. The others have dowel at both ends, so they can be placed in the clamping slots during the final assembly of the guitar, when the clamping blocks are not in use. Note also the two yoke pieces which are used to apply pressure to the heel of the neck and to the bottom block. These are threaded onto two of the spool clamps and tightened down with washers and wing nuts.

8 An inspection hole allows you to view the inside of the guitar after the back has been attached. This is accomplished by cutting out a circular plug concentric with the soundhole. This plug has to be replaceable, so that the centre of the soundhole can be located on the solera in the early stages of construction. Mark the exact centre of the soundhole, and draw a circle of about 4½in (115mm) diameter on the underside of the board. Drill a ⅛in (3mm) hole through the face of the solera in the centre of the soundhole location. Screw a 1 x 2in (25 x 50mm) hardwood batten over the hole, with two screws inside the circle and another two outside; make sure the screws do not go all the way through the solera. Working from the front of the solera and using a 4½in (115mm) holesaw, cut through the plywood, using the ⅛in (3mm) hole as a pilot, but do not cut through the hardwood batten. Now all you need to do to see inside the guitar is to remove the two outer screws and lift out the plug.

2 THE NECK AND ENDBLOCK

The neck components assembled and awaiting final shaping

The neck of a guitar has to be light and rigid, remaining flat along and across its surface. It must be able to pass some of the string vibrations back into the body of the guitar, and may need to be of a small cross-section to suit a player with small hands. This is quite a lot to ask!

The neck is attached to the body by one of two methods. One is to use a tenon formed on the heel end of the neck, inserted into a socket cut in the body of the guitar. The tenon can be dovetailed or square; if square, it is screwed or bolted from the inside. One maker includes a screw adjuster that allows the angle of the neck joint to be changed while the strings are still in place.

The alternative method, which we will employ, entails the neck and heel being glued to the soundboard first, and the ribs being let into slots cut in the sides of the neck.

When you receive the neck blank from the supplier it will have a rough-sawn finish. It may come in a single piece measuring about 36 x 3 x 1⅛in (910 x 75 x 28mm), or in two pieces, approximately 24in (610mm) long for the neck blank and 12in (305mm) for the heel and standard endblock. (The instructions below assume a single piece.) If you want to make the improved endblock described at the end of this chapter, you will

MATERIALS

For neck and standard endblock:
- Mahogany, 36 x 3 x 1⅛in (910 x 75 x 28mm) (can be in two pieces, 24 and 12in (610 and 305mm) long)
- Truss rod (see page 38)
- Ebony offcut, 3in (75mm) x width and depth of truss rod
- Hardwood strip, 24 x ⅛in (610 x 3mm) x width of truss rod
- Ebony or other decorative hardwood for head veneer, 6 x 3½ x ⅛in (150 x 90 x 3mm); additional contrasting veneers if desired

For improved endblock (see page 57):
6 x 3 x 1⅜in (150 x 75 x 35mm)

TIP

The full-size plans are for a guitar of 25½in (648mm) scale length with 14 frets to the body. If you prefer to make a 12-fret model, you will need to recalculate the scale length and neck length accordingly.

require the additional piece listed above. The completed neck and heel will look better if all pieces are cut from the same piece of timber, so the colour and grain match.

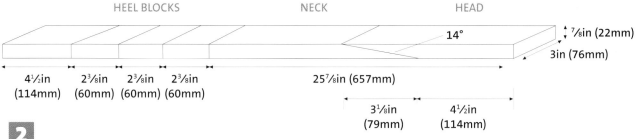

HEEL BLOCKS				NECK	HEAD

14°

⁷⁄₈in (22mm)

3in (76mm)

4¹⁄₂in
(114mm)   2³⁄₈in   2³⁄₈in   2³⁄₈in   25⁷⁄₈in (657mm)
(60mm)   (60mm)   (60mm)

3¹⁄₈in
(79mm)   4¹⁄₂in
(114mm)

TIP

For ease of handling and marking out, leave the sides of the neck parallel for as long as possible – certainly until after the guitar body has been assembled. This allows it to be held in the vice without difficulty, and also protects the edges from damage while you are working on the body.

MAKING THE NECK BLANK

1 Start by thicknessing the neck and heel blocks to 1in (25mm) and squaring the edges parallel, as close as possible to 3in (76mm) wide. Draw a centre line on top, bottom and end surfaces.

2 Mark out the neck as shown in the sketch (which is not to scale). The diagonal line for the head joint is at 14°, which will give the correct neck-to-head angle when reversed and glued.

3 As each piece is cut, mark it for correct orientation. If you intend to finish the neck with a light-coloured stain, it is important to stack and glue the heel blocks in the order in which they were cut. When they are glued together and shaped, it should look as though the heel and neck have been cut from a single piece of timber.

4 Glue and clamp the heel blocks tightly together using plywood cauls and polythene sheet each side. I clamp the whole assembly in the main bench vice, as it provides equal pressure over the whole of the gluing surface. Care needs to be taken when applying the clamping pressure, as the wet glue can act as a lubricant, allowing the blocks to slide out of alignment.

5&6 While the glued heel blocks are in the clamps, you can make a start on the neck and head joint. Cut the head timber off the remaining piece of neck blank at the marked angle of 14°. Any less, and the angle of the strings over the top nut will be insufficient to give a clear, crisp sound to the guitar; any more, and your guitar will start to look like a lute. The two photos show how the head piece, after planing, will be turned over and reattached to the back of the neck.

7 The final thickness of the head needs to be about ⅝in (15mm), but first check this against the machine tuners you intend to use. Subtract the thickness of your selected head-veneer sandwich from the required final thickness of the head, and plane the head block down to this thickness either now or when the veneers are ready.

MATERIALS

For the scarf-planing clamp:

- Two hardwood strips, ¾ x 2 x 6in (19 x 50 x 150mm)
- Two lengths of threaded rod, 5/16 x 6in (M8 x 150mm), with two washers and two wing nuts to match
- Prepared hardwood, 3 x 4 x 24in (75 x 100 x 610mm)

8 When planing the scarf for the neck-to-head joint, I support the pieces on a substantial piece of timber held in the main bench vice. I made the scarf-planing clamp from two pieces of ash, but oak or other hardwood would work just as well. The upper piece has holes drilled and tapped to fit the threaded rod (it is best if these holes do not go all the way through, so the plane blade cannot catch on the rod); the lower piece has clearance holes. Apply some wood glue to the ends of the threaded rods and screw them into the tapped holes, slide the other timber over the ends and fit the washers and wing nuts.

9 The neck and head can now be planed together, to ensure a matching angle. It helps if the end of the supporting timber is shaped to the same 14° angle.

MATERIALS

For the neck-clamping workboard:

- Plywood, ³⁄₄in x 3 x 30in (19 x 75 x 760mm)
- Scrap wood, 1 x 2 x 12in (25 x 50 x 305mm)
- Scrap wood, 1 x 2 x 4in (25 x 50 x 100mm)
- 4 plywood cauls, ¹⁄₄ x 2 x 3in (6 x 50 x 75mm)
- Plastic packing tape
- Woodscrews and glue

10 The neck and head timbers are assembled on another workboard, made from plywood with a batten screwed and glued to its underside. (I prefer to remove the screws after the glue has set.) The top face of the plywood is covered with brown plastic packing tape to act as a non-stick surface, as are the cauls. I clamp this workboard in an engineer's vice.

Clamp the neck block to the plywood, making sure the face of the neck timber is at 90° to the workboard. Fit the head block to the neck block and adjust the positioning until the thickness of the joint equals that of the head block; visually check that there is no step in the joint. Clamp a small piece of scrap timber on the end to prevent the head block from slipping during the gluing process; this piece, seen on the far right of the photo, has a notch cut in it to engage the end of the head.

Apply a thin coat of your chosen glue to both surfaces, gently press them together and clamp, using the plywood cauls. Clean up the excess glue and leave to set. Long-reach clamps are extremely helpful here.

11 When the glue has dried and set, remove the clamps and clean up. Lightly plane the top face of the head, making sure you do not go below the thickness you established earlier. When the scarf joint has been cleaned of surplus glue, redraw the centre line on the neck and head, continuing down the end and onto the underside of the head.

12 Glue the heel-block assembly to the neck, making sure that heel and neck are in line. When the glue has dried and set, clean up and smooth the back face of the heel block with a file, and mark out down the centre line of the neck for the truss-rod installation.

INSTALLING THE TRUSS ROD

13 Having chosen your truss rod (see page 38), rout out a snug groove just deep and wide enough for it to sit in. Be aware of the final thickness of the neck, and don't go too deep with the truss-rod groove.

14 The truss rod needs to be inserted with a slight slope, so as to allow the adjusting nut to clear the soundboard and bracing inside the body of the completed guitar. At the head end it lies at the surface of the neck, so as not to weaken the joint, while at the body end it should lie ⅛in (3mm) below the surface. The depth and width of the slot can be fine-tuned by using a scraper, or a credit-card-sized piece of plastic covered with abrasive paper. Be careful: at the lower end of the neck, near the heel, there is at most ¼in (6mm) clearance between the underside of the truss rod and the back surface of the neck.

TRUSS-ROD ADJUSTMENT

In most acoustic guitars the adjustment for the truss rod is made from inside the body. Some manufacturers have the adjustment nut under a small plate on the head of the guitar; though this makes it easier to adjust, it will weaken the head-to-neck joint. It is legitimate when you do not have easy access to the inside of the body – as in some mandolins, for instance – or in solid-body electrics where the neck otherwise has to be removed to make the adjustment.

15 Place the truss rod in the slot. It should be a snug fit, but is not glued, for fear of gumming up the threads. If the routed slot extends onto the head, glue in a piece of ebony scrap to fill in the end of the slot and possibly add some strength.

16 With the truss rod in place, glue in a cover strip made from an offcut of hardwood. When the glue has set, plane the strip flush; there will be nothing left of it at the top end, where the truss rod is flush with the surface.

17 Carefully redraw the centre line and mark the position of the nut, exactly at right angles to the centre line of the neck.

SHAPING THE HEEL END

18 Referring to the full-size plans, mark out the shape of the heel and the rib positions. On a standard guitar, the ribs fit into sawn slots in either side of the heel, but for a cutaway model the heel must be made asymmetrical, the rib on the treble side being glued into a shallow rebate. In my design the bass rib enters the neck at 90°, giving a squarish look to the shoulder of the guitar; if a more rounded shape is preferred, the slot for the rib will have to be cut at a slight angle. Start by measuring from the fretboard side of the top nut the required distance back to the 14th fret, which corresponds with the neck–body joint; for the model shown, this distance is 14.15in (359.35mm).

TIP

If you clamp a long steel rule to the face of the neck at the heel end, you can easily bend it so as to extend the centre line of the neck onto the head.

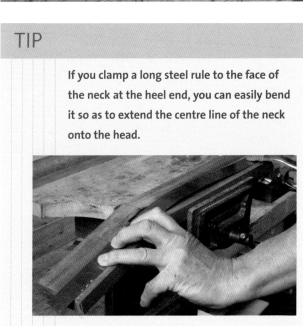

Draw a line all round the neck at this point, then add a second line ⁵⁄₆₄in (2mm) back from the first to mark the position of the inside of the rib. (For a cutaway model, this second line is needed on the bass side only.)

19 Referring to the plans, mark on the heel the centre line of the instrument and the width of the heel at both front and back; remember that the side of the heel will taper towards the back, on the bass side only.

20 Carefully join up your marks at front and back, so the slope of the bass side is clearly shown on the rear face of the heel.

ACCOMMODATING THE CUTAWAY

For a symmetrical-bodied guitar, the heel is tapered uniformly on both sides. When making a guitar with a cutaway, only the bass side of the heel is tapered; the treble side is left square, so the cutaway rib lies flat against the side of the heel block.

End view of the completed heel, showing how the bass side slopes and the cutaway side does not

21 To cut the rib slots in the neck, I use a modified tenon saw with the teeth set to give a kerf ⁵⁄₆₄in (2mm) wide. Alternative solutions would be to make a handsaw from part of an old industrial hacksaw blade – these come with fine teeth and a wide kerf – or to tape several hacksaw blades together to make up the required width. Measure the depth of the slot from the full-size drawing and mark this carefully before cutting. Remember that the cutaway side needs only a shallow rebate instead of a slot; make a shallow saw cut, then chisel out the rebate to the thickness of the rib.

22 With the rib slots cut, you can now saw off the waste wood from the part of the heel block that will be inside the guitar body.

23 The part that will be inside is now tidied up using chisels, violin planes and files, as convenient. The protruding tongue or 'slipper block' is gracefully tapered as shown, and the edges on the bass side are neatly rounded over; the cutaway side, to which the treble-side rib will be glued, is left square. Apply one coat of sanding sealer to keep out moisture.

Note that in this picture a small part of the neck adjacent to the body joint has been cut approximately to width on the bandsaw, to provide a little more working space. The bulk of the neck is still left square at this stage.

24 Where the neck meets the soundboard it is necessary to cut a ledge into the neck equal to the final thickness of the soundboard. Make a shallow saw cut exactly in line with the rib slot, then pare the rebate for the soundboard in the same way as you did for the rib on the cutaway side.

THE HEAD

25 Prepare a cardboard template for the head outline. The pattern shown here is fairly wide, and necessitates building up the width of the neck blank by gluing on two 'ears' at the sides; make these from offcuts of the same wood, and match the grain direction of the head as closely as possible. For a slimmer style these extra pieces would not be necessary.

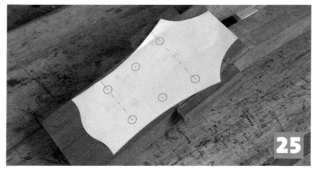

HEAD DESIGN

If you prefer to design your own head shape, you need to be aware of the placement of the machine tuners and how the strings lead onto the posts from the top nut. Before you settle on the final shape, draw it out full size on a piece of paper, marking the locations and diameters of the tuner posts. Mark the string locations on the top nut, then draw the strings; watch out for the strings rubbing against the adjacent posts.

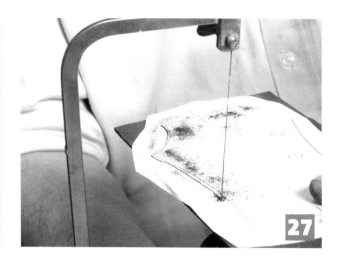

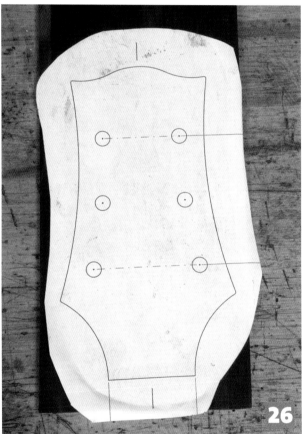

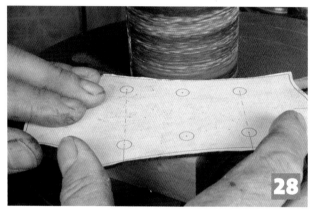

26 Select your head veneer and glue a photocopied paper template to it. The veneer shown here is a single layer of ebony, to which inlaid bindings will later be added. An alternative treatment is to use multiple layers of contrasting veneers, which will show as fine stripes around the edges of the head; typically this would be the top hardwood veneer at $\frac{7}{64}$in (2.75mm) thick, plus two or three contrasting colours.

27 & 28 The head veneer is cut to shape with a piercing saw, then the curved outline is refined on the drum sander.

29 Measure the thickness of the head, and reduce it (if you have not already done so) so that once the vencer (or veneer sandwich) has been added the overall thickness will suit your chosen machine tuners.

30 To prevent the veneer from slipping, you could insert a couple of small panel pins through holes drilled at the tuner locations. Then, with the neck clamped in the vice, paint the veneer and the front of the head with glue, and lay the veneer on the head. Place a small piece of polythene over the veneer, followed by plywood cauls top and bottom, and carefully tighten the clamps.

31 When the glue has set and dried, drill the holes to suit the barrels of your chosen tuners. A pillar drill gives the most accurate results.

32 Using blocks to support the work at the correct angle on the bandsaw table, trim the softer mahogany back to the line of the ebony veneer. Finish with the drum sander, or by scraping with a cabinet scraper or a razor blade. Scrape off the paper pattern once you have finished with it.

33 The final task is to trim the back edge square to the centre line and at 90° to the neck surface, to form a support for the top nut. This can be done with a file or a home-made sanding stick, as here. Apply one coat of sanding sealer to keep the head clean.

THE ENDBLOCK

34 The endblock serves to connect the two ribs at the end of the guitar body, and to provide a secure fixing for the back and soundboard at this vital point. A simple endblock (shown on the left in the photo) consists of a piece of timber 4 x 3 x 1in (100 x 75 x 25mm) with the vertical inside corners rounded over. One drawback of this type of block is that it offers end grain as a gluing surface for the back and soundboard. This problem is obviated by the alternative design shown on the right, which features two endcaps whose grain runs at right angles to that of the main block. This substantial block can be carved to reduce weight without sacrificing strength.

Plane the faces clean and edges square. Cut the blocks to the dimensions given in the plans and glue the top and bottom keyed timbers to the body block, clamp tightly and leave till the glue has set.

35 The side which will face the inside of the guitar is dished as shown in the side elevation drawing.

36 In plan view, the block is now sawn to an ogee shape.

37 If you plan to fit a pickup jack, you will need to create a flat spot in the middle of the block face for the jack to seat against. I use a 1in (25mm) Forstner bit to create a round flat surface in the middle of the block.

When done, sand smooth and apply a couple of coats of sanding sealer.

3 THE SOUNDBOARD

The soundboard can be thought of as the engine of the guitar, and as such needs to be tuned to its maximum potential to get the best sound from the instrument. Use only good-quality timber: straight-grained, quartersawn, with narrow annual rings and without knots, resin pockets or other flaws.

MATERIALS

- Bookmatched spruce soundboard timber, 20 x 16 x ³⁄₁₆in (510 x 410 x 5mm)
- Sitka spruce for braces (see plans, and page 70)
- Maple or other hardwood for bridge backing plate, 6 x 2 x ³⁄₁₆in (150 x 50 x 5mm)
- Soundhole inlay of your choice (see pages 61–5)

The soundboard with inlay completed, ready for cutting out the soundhole

JOINTING THE SOUNDBOARD

1 If the boards are still in a rough-sawn condition, plane off some of the surface on both sides to reveal the grain direction. The supplier will normally have marked the boards at the matching edges, and may have drawn a guitar body outline suggesting which part of the board to use. Laying the two halves side by side on the bench, check that the tighter grain runs down the joining edge and that there is little or no grain runout over the length of the joint – that is, the grain is parallel to the centre join. If not, you will need to adjust the angle at which the two plates meet, and plane the edges of the boards to bring the grain parallel.

2 Clamp the soundboard halves on a shooting board with the jointing edge hanging over just enough to reveal the rough edges of the plates, then allow the plane to work down to a smooth, straight, square edge. Start by taking a coarse cut to remove the saw marks, then progress by taking finer cuts till the plane just whispers as it is pushed along the edge. To check how good the joint is, remove the clamps and hold up the two plates edge to edge in front of a bright light; you should not see any light between the edges of the plates. If there are gaps in the seam you will see slivers of light showing through; in which case, return the plates to the shooting board and, taking finer cuts, work till there is no light showing at the seam.

3 Parcel tape can be used to hold the plates together. Fold them back to expose the meeting edges, and apply glue to both edges of the plates. The two plates can then be laid on the workboard and held down with weights, or clamped between battens as shown. Alternatively, fasten two battens along the outside edges of the workboard and use small wedges to press the plates together, again using weights to hold them down. If you have planed the edges properly, you should only need a slight tap with a pin hammer to seat the wedges; over-wedging will not correct a badly planed joint.

THE SHOOTING BOARD

As shown in photo 2, this simple planing aid consists of two layers of plywood, the lower layer projecting beyond the upper one to provide a support for the plane laid on its side. A stop is fixed across the end at right angles, and a batten underneath enables the whole device to be held in the bench vice.

4 When the glue has dried and set, remove the tape or wedges, and carefully prise the soundboard from the workboard or battens. Be extremely careful, as sometimes the glue will have stuck the soundboard to the tape on the workboard. Now clamp the soundboard back onto the workboard for planing. I use plastic-faced spring clamps; if you are using G-cramps (C-clamps), always use a piece of clean, smooth ply to protect the soundboard surface. Carefully plane the glue joint, then scrape or sand the whole surface smooth, reversing direction as necessary to work with the grain.

Once both sides have been cleaned up in this way, inspect the soundboard and decide which will be the outside face. If you have achieved a perfect centre seam, the glue line will be difficult to see, so, once you have identified it, mark the centre line on both ends and both faces of the soundboard, just a little way in from the end.

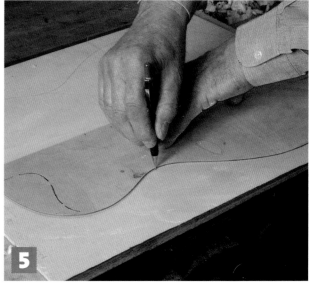

5 Place the template on the soundboard and mark the position of the centre of the soundhole. Draw the body outline just as you did on the solera; the method of drawing the cutaway was shown on page 42, step 2.

MAKING THE SOUNDHOLE INLAY

6 Draw the soundhole circle, as well as the surrounding circles of decorative inlay. These will be used as a reference for positioning the inlay. Drill a locating hole exactly in the centre of the soundhole, to suit the pin of the hole-cutting tool that you are going to use. This hole will also be used to locate the soundhole backing plate.

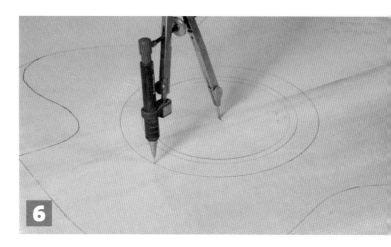

6

7 The main ring of the rosette for this instrument is made from burr (burl) walnut veneer about 1⁄16in (1.5mm) thick, laminated if necessary between two thick plywood cauls. A hole is drilled in the centre to take the pin of the circle cutter, which in my case is a miniature electric router mounted on a specially made trammel base. The pin is fixed through the veneer into the plywood workboard.

7

TIP

Before you actually rout or inlay the soundboard, try the process on a piece of scrap timber, such as clear, tight-grained pine.

8 The outside diameter of the walnut disc is cut first, taking a series of gentle, shallow passes with the router.

8

9 Thick polythene sheeting is placed beneath the veneer to prevent it sticking to the workboard. A length of black–white–black purfling, either bought or home-made, is cut a little longer than the circumference of the walnut disc, and its end is mitred with either scalpel or chisel.

TIP

If you polish the chisel, the reflection of the purfling in the blade should help you judge the correct angle: when the purfling and its reflection appear at 90° to each other, the blade will cut a 45° mitre.

VENEER STRIPS

You can buy veneer inlay strips already cut, or make your own. The standard thickness of most veneers is 0.02in (0.5mm). I start by cutting the veneer sheets up into strips of about 20 x 2½in (500 x 60mm). Where I require thinner sections, I take the large strips and sand them down to the required thickness in a home-made thickness sander, which is based on a sanding drum fitted to the drill press. I use the miniature circular saw shown on page 17 to cut up the veneer strips; a small piece of timber screwed to the fence prevents the veneer from lifting and fouling the blade.

Veneers accurately sanded to 0.012in (0.3 mm) are available from luthier suppliers, but they are quite expensive and colours are limited.

9

10

11

10 The purfling is eased into position around the edge of the walnut disc, and superglue (cyanoacrylate) is applied to bond the two together.

11 The other end of the purfling is mitred as before, to provide as accurate a join as possible. Once set, the ring of purfling will stabilize the walnut veneer and help to resist distortion as work proceeds. Use a block plane to bring the purfling down flush with the walnut.

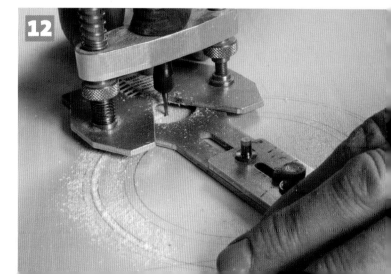

12

12 The soundboard is now returned to the workboard, and the miniature router is used to cut the outermost edge of the recess for the rosette to a depth of ¹⁄₁₆in (1.5mm).

13 A second strip of black–white–black is inlaid into this groove, the ends mitred as before. It is superglued in place and planed down flush with the soundboard.

14 A narrow band of light-coloured veneer will be inserted between the two rows of purfling. Try this for size now; it can then be scraped thinner if necessary. It should fit quite tightly, but without causing any distortion.

15 The recess in the soundboard is now widened to the full width of the inlay. Work inwards, adjusting the trammel setting in small increments and being careful to cut no deeper than ¹⁄₁₆in (1.5mm).

16 The rest of the inlay is completed using the same techniques. The hole in the walnut disc is cut out very carefully with the router, and a line of purfling is glued around the inside of it. A fourth row of purfling is applied to the inside edge of the routed recess, and a second band of light-coloured veneer is prepared to fit between the two inner rows of purfling. All the parts are then glued in place with the aid of weights, using plastic sheeting to prevent any unwanted bonding. When set, the inlay is cleaned up and given a coat of sealer. Be careful when sanding or scraping inlaid veneers, as they can tear and leave micro-pockets that trap dark-coloured wood, causing a smudgy look when the finish is applied.

17 When the sealer has dried, cut the soundhole halfway through, working from the outside face. Do not cut all the way through at this stage: the completion of the soundhole will be done from the inside, after the backing plate has been attached. The hole in the middle will be needed to locate the soundhole backing plate prior to gluing.

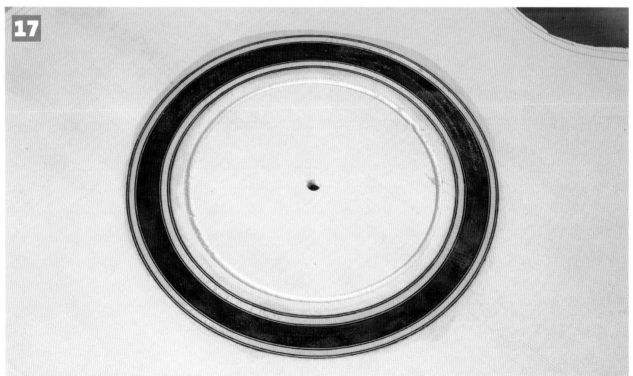

CUTTING OUT AND THICKNESSING

18 Place the template on the centre line of the soundboard and line up the soundhole position and the centre line of the soundboard. Holding the template steady, draw the outline onto the soundboard.

19 Now draw a second outline parallel to the first but about ⁵⁄₃₂in (4mm) outside it, by placing the pencil inside a washer of suitable size. The excess will be used for clamping the soundboard to the solera.

20 Using a coping saw, cut out the soundboard on the *outer* line, then clean the edges with sandpaper.

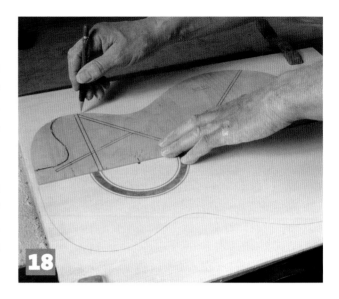

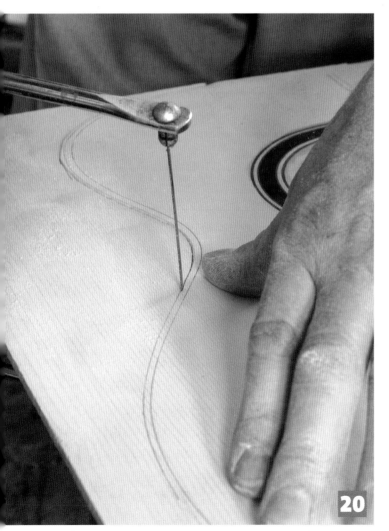

RESPONSIVENESS

For the guitar to have good sound projection, sustain and volume, the soundboard needs to be light and responsive. A good guitar should 'say hello' to you when you walk into the room. By that I mean that the sound of the door being opened and your footsteps crossing the floor should be picked up by the soundboard and transferred to the strings, making them vibrate – providing the guitar is not still in its case, that is.

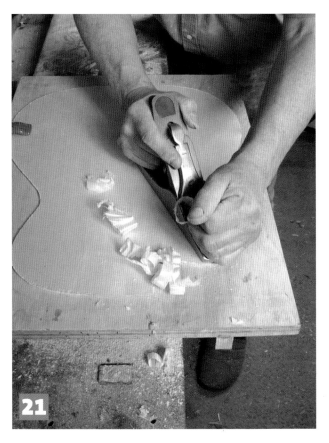

23 You can leave the soundboard at these dimensions or you can continue to tune it for optimum response, by a process called 'tap-tuning'. The following information can serve only as a guide. Basically, each piece of wood has its own tonal qualities and responses to vibration. Some locations of the soundboard have almost no vibrations, and these areas are called 'node points'. To find the node point on your soundboard, experiment by holding the soundboard on the edge, between the upper bout and the waist. Hold the soundboard lightly at the node point with your middle finger and thumb, and hold it to your ear as you tap the bridge or centre areas. By trial and error you will hear the optimum place to hold the soundboard. The sound generated should be bright and clear, like the sound made when you tap a piece of plate glass suspended in the air. There are papers written on the subject of tap-tuning, and if you wish to study the matter further, an Internet search will provide you with many hours of esoteric reading.

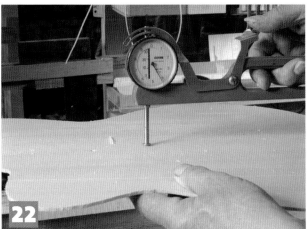

21 & 22 Dust off the workboard and clamp the soundboard face down. A useful additional holding aid is a small wooden dowel, inserted through the hole at the soundboard centre and trimmed off flush. Plane the surface of the soundboard down to about ⅛in (3mm) all over, then sand or scrape to a constant ³⁄₃₂in (2.5mm) in the centre, grading down to ⁵⁄₆₄in (2mm) at the edge; when complete, redraw the outline using the template.

TUNING THE SOUNDBOARD

Soundboard tuning is a deep subject, with many builders having their own opinions and approaches. Some use a sound generator, which causes the soundboard, clamped by one edge, to vibrate while fine-grained sand is spread on it to show the areas of vibration relating to the different frequencies. But tap-tuning is the usual method.

24

SOUNDBOARD BRACING

24 For the soundhole backing plate, select a piece of tight, vertical-grained spruce that when cut into a circle will have a diameter at least ⅛in (3mm) greater than the soundhole inlay. Leave it about ⁵⁄₆₄in (2mm) thick at this stage. Drill a hole in the centre for the circle cutter, place the spruce on the workboard and cut out the circle using the same method as before.

Lift off the backing plate and position the soundboard on the workboard, with the circle-cutter pin through the hole in the centre of the soundhole. Cut a plywood caul the same diameter as the backing plate, and drill a hole in the middle. Apply glue to the backing plate and seat it over the soundboard, ensuring that its grain is at 90° to that of the soundboard.

ORDER OF ASSEMBLY

1 Soundhole backing plate
2 X-brace
3 Bridge backing plate
4 Lower harmonic bars
5 Wing harmonic bars
6 Upper A-braces
7 Upper-bout spreader bar

TIP

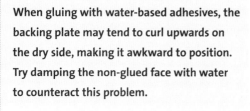

When gluing with water-based adhesives, the backing plate may tend to curl upwards on the dry side, making it awkward to position. Try damping the non-glued face with water to counteract this problem.

25 Lay a piece of polythene over the plate and cover with the plywood caul. Either clamp, or place heavy weights on top till the glue has set. Before the glue has cured fully, remove the caul and polythene so you can clean up the excess glue; then replace the caul and weights and leave to cure.

26 When set, remove the caul and plane the backing plate down to about ⅟₁₆in (1.5mm) thick. Finish by slightly bevelling the edge and sanding the plate smooth.

27 Turn the soundboard over and reset the circle cutter to the soundhole diameter by using the partially cut groove for reference. Make sure that the soundboard face and the workboard are spotlessly clean, and relocate the soundboard face down on the workboard by using the circle-cutting pin as before. Carefully fix the soundboard to the workboard using clamps and cauls. Complete the cutting out of the soundhole from the inside. Because you previously cut halfway through from the outside, you will not need to go all the way through this time. Cutting from both sides prevents splintering on the edge as the cutter breaks through. Do not round over the edge of the hole yet; this will be done when it is prepared for finishing.

GRAIN ORIENTATION

It is important to orientate the grain in the bracing vertically for maximum strength. A good way of achieving this is to saw or split the brace material from a wedge-shaped quartersawn blank intended for a violin or cello soundboard.

28 The X-brace is the framework that supports the vibrating soundboard, much as the main spar in an aircraft wing supports the substructure of the wing. It needs to be strong and light, to accept high-frequency vibrations without disintegrating and without damping the vibrations, and to withstand a wide range of temperatures and changes in humidity.

Select two pieces of straight, vertical-grained spruce 1 x ¼ x 22in (25 x 6 x 560mm) and mark out the notches for a half-lap joint 9in (230mm) from what will be the upper end of each brace. Cut and dry-fit the two pieces; they should be a snug fit, and for this design they should meet at 90°.

29 Glue the two pieces together, using right-angled clamping blocks as shown; alternatively, place them on the bench with a weight to hold them down.

Material for guitar braces cut from a wedge-shaped piece of quartersawn spruce

30 When the glue has dried, clean the corners and glue in filler blocks ³⁄₁₆in (5mm) square. When these are set, use a small gouge to carve a smooth transition radius in the corners, and sand smooth.

31 To make the soundboard light and responsive we will start by building a curve into the face of it. We do this by carving the face of the X-brace to match the depression already formed in the solera, so that the curve of the soundboard will be held in place by the curvature of the X-brace. Lay the X-brace in its correct position on the solera and scribe the curve as shown, again using a washer to provide the necessary offset.

32 Carefully plane down to the line, making sure that the curve is fair and that the X-brace sits flat on the solera.

TIP

Mark the flat side of the X-brace with a coloured spot so that you can easily distinguish it from the side that has been shaped to fit the solera.

TIP

Before fitting any of the braces, accurately re-mark the outline and centre line of the soundboard, which will have been obliterated when the soundboard was reduced to thickness.

34 Clamp the soundboard to the solera, making sure that their centre lines match and that the lines of the upper bout, waist and lower bout line up with the lines drawn on the solera. Lay the X-brace in position, aligning the top end of each brace with the position of the upper-bout spreader bar, and draw round it. Draw in the positions of the remaining braces by reference to the full-size plan. You will see that the X-brace, the A-braces and the upper-bout spreader bar all impinge on the soundhole backing plate, which has to be cut out to receive them.

33 To aid in getting a perfect fit, lay a piece of sandpaper grit-side up on the solera and work it back and forward to remove the high spots on the brace. A simple spool clamp can be used to secure the brace to the solera during this operation.

35 Mark out the recesses in the backing plate with a scalpel first, then cut with a fine backsaw and carefully pare out the waste with a chisel. Use a violin plane to feather the edge of the backing plate in the areas where it has not been cut away for the braces.

36 You may like to run strips of low-tack masking tape down each side of the X-brace location; this aids in cleaning up excess glue and keeps the soundboard clean. My preferred method of clamping the braces to the soundboard while gluing is to use the go-bar frame described on page 19. The X-brace needs to be glued on first, as it establishes the domed shape of the soundboard. Place your first go-bar on the centre of the X, making sure that it has pressed both the X-brace and the soundboard firmly onto the solera. Continue to place the remainder of the go-bars (you may have to recheck the previous ones as you go), then check that the X-brace arms are straight and haven't moved out of position. Once clamped, removed any squeezed-out glue with a stick or bamboo skewer sharpened to a chisel point.

37 Mark the undulating shape of the X-braces using templates, and carefully pare them to shape with a chisel. Finish with a violin plane and sandpaper.

ALTERNATIVE CLAMPING METHODS

Some guitar factories use vacuum-forming techniques in which the braces are held down onto the soundboard under a flexible membrane. A vacuum is drawn, pulling the membrane down and holding the braces against the soundboard till the glue sets. A similar method is used in commercial veneering, and home-made adaptations have been devised.

Another alternative to the go-bar method employs long-reach clamps made of cast aluminium, forged steel or wood.

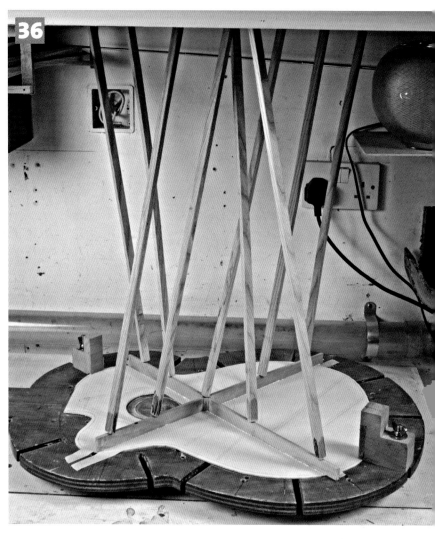

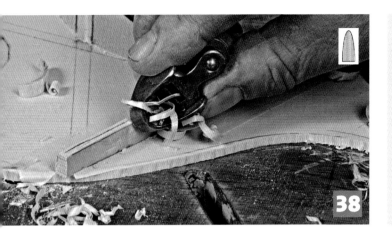

LIGHTENING THE LOAD

Carving and shaping the braces reduces the sprung weight of the soundboard, and a lighter soundboard is a more responsive soundboard, giving good separation of the notes and controllable sustain. Also, having less of the string energy consumed in making the soundboard vibrate allows for a more sensitive playing style.

38 You can leave the braces square, but it is customary to round the edges, often to a parabolic profile as shown inset.

39 The bridge backing plate, shown here complete, takes the tension of the ball ends of the strings. It is normally made from hardwood such as maple. Make it to the size shown in the plans, then adjust it to fit as snugly as possible to the soundboard and X-braces, before gluing to the soundboard. When the glue has set, remove the go-bars, carefully round over the edges and sand everything smooth.

40 Prepare the rest of the braces in the same way, referring to the plans for their size, position and shaping, and glue on the lower braces, followed by the small wing braces and, next to last, the A-braces. These are the only ones that butt up against the X-braces – sometimes they are housed

or recessed into the X-braces – and their upper ends, which are left square, go into sockets carved in the neck block when the neck is fitted. A credit-card-sized piece of plastic, cut from an old lunchbox, protects the X-brace from damage as the wing braces and lower braces are carved to shape.

BUILDING FOR THE FUTURE

Over a period of years the bridge plate suffers from the wear of the strings being removed and refitted, so it is a good idea to be kind to future repairers and use animal glue if you can. This will enable the plate to be removed and replaced when the need arises, without damaging the underside of the soundboard.

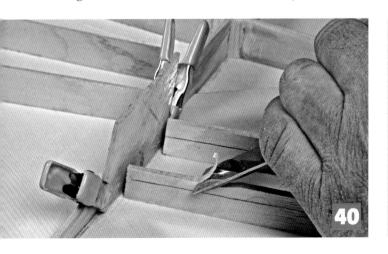

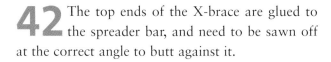

41 The last brace to be fitted is the upper-bout spreader bar. This has two arches carved and rounded into it where the A-braces pass through, and is reduced height in the middle to allow the truss-rod adjuster key to fit. The arches are cut with a Forstner bit; the photograph shows them being tested for fit, with the upper edge of the bar still to be smoothed.

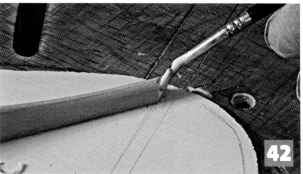

42 The top ends of the X-brace are glued to the spreader bar, and need to be sawn off at the correct angle to butt against it.

43 Finally, glue two small diamond-shaped buttons of ¹⁄₁₆in (1.5mm) spruce on the centre line, as shown on the plans, and a small rectangular patch of the same material adjacent to the neck. These all contribute to reinforcing the centre seam.

4 RIBS AND LININGS

The completed pair of ribs, with the linings fitted on the soundboard side

Probably your most labour-intensive task will be thicknessing and bending the ribs and preparing the back plates. Choose reasonably plain wood for your first instrument; this will bend more easily than highly figured wood, and be less expensive to replace if you do happen to make an irretrievable mistake.

Both ribs and back are bookmatched, and matched back and ribs are often sold together as a set. Some suppliers will coarse-sand them to your desired thickness. If you are having this done, ask them to leave enough thickness to permit cleaning up the surfaces after bending – you must be able to remove any scorch marks left from the bending operation and still have enough thickness left. Before bending, the ribs need to be reduced to about ⁵⁄₆₄in (2mm) thick – or slightly less in the area of the cutaway – and the back plates to about ³⁄₃₂in (2.5mm).

MATERIALS

- Bookmatched pair of rosewood ribs, each 36 x 5 x ¹⁄₈in (915 x 127 x 3mm)
- Willow for linings: 4 pieces 36 x ³⁄₄ x ⁵⁄₃₂in (915 x 19 x 4mm)

TIP

Undoubtedly the hardest part of bending the ribs is negotiating the tight curves in the cutaway area. If you find this daunting, you can make life much easier for yourself by building your first instrument with a symmetrical outline instead, and saving the cutaway style for when you have gained a little more experience.

PLANING THIN WOOD

Very thin wood necessitates special methods of working, especially when it is too narrow to be clamped easily. Unless it is held in tension, a long, thin guitar rib can buckle, and even break, when the plane is pushed along it. One suggestion is to place several short lengths of double-sided tape underneath the wood to hold it down. Another method, if the wood is to be scraped rather than planed, is to place it on a workboard and grip one end with a small spring clamp, allowing the scraper to be worked away from the clamp. Having tried whether the wood will plane easily or not, you can decide whether to plane or scrape it down to final thickness.

PREPARING THE RIBS

1 Before you thickness the ribs, the edge which will be glued to the soundboard must be planed square and straight on the shooting board. (The back edge need not be planed until after the ribs have been glued to the soundboard and the linings attached.)

2 The inside faces are worked next. Start by inspecting the wood to determine the grain direction, as tear-outs caused by planing the wrong way cannot be rectified easily. A very sharp plane is necessary for this operation.

3 Plane, sand and scrape the outside of both ribs flat and smooth, down to the final thickness of ⁵⁄₆₄in (2mm), and mark the inside faces. Make sure there are no plane marks left, as this can cause local stress areas and result in splits when the rib is bent. The finish is not important at this time: the process of bending the ribs causes the oils in the wood to come out, and this may blacken the surface, necessitating refinishing later.

TIP

The body of the guitar tapers in depth from the bottom end to the neck, as shown in the plans. Some rib timber when supplied can be undersize, so it is useful to inform your supplier of the required sizes when you order. When ordering by post, it is advisable to send a full-size paper template of the ribs and the soundboard or back.

A SANDING PLANE

A sanding plane, easily made from stout plywood, makes light work of sanding the ribs to thickness.

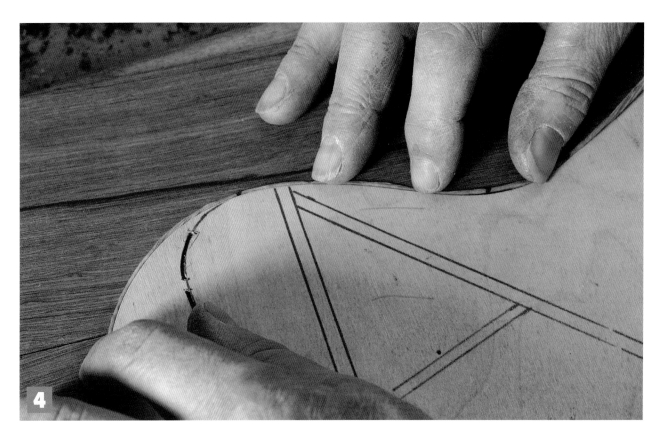

4 Lay the body template on the bench. Take a short length of waxed twine and, starting from the neck end, carefully lay it round the perimeter of the template. (It takes a little practice to get this right.) Using a dark-coloured, medium-tipped marker pen, place bold dots on the string at the upper bout, waist, lower bout and the centre line at both ends.

5 Now lay the string straight along the ribs and transfer the marked positions to the outsides of the ribs using a white wax pencil or a typist's correction pen. This will make it much easier to see where the bending positions are when you start to bend the ribs; sometimes the oils of the wood and the water applied to the surface combine to make it difficult to see where you are.

BENDING THE RIBS

6 While the bending iron (see page 16) is warming up, prepare your bending former or mould and its associated clamping blocks. As explained on page 27, the former has inter-changeable inserts allowing it to be used for both sides of the cutaway guitar body; separate clamping blocks will be needed for each insert.

7 Have a dry run with the clamping blocks, to ensure that the clamps are correctly adjusted before you need to use them.

8 Some woods can be bent dry, but most – including the brittle rosewoods – need to be wetted before bending.

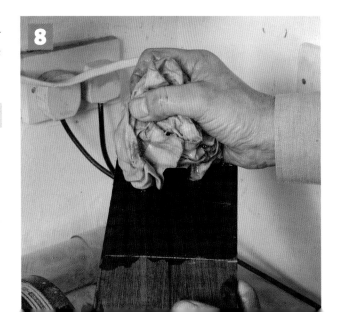

WARNING

A lot of very hot steam is generated in the bending process, so you may want to use protective gloves to prevent burns to your hands.

9 Bend the bass-side rib first, so you will not have to tackle the cutaway until you have got into your stride. Remind yourself which is the outside surface, and which edge will be joined to the soundboard; in the photographs, the white pencil marks are on the outside, and the soundboard edge is marked with an arrow.

Start at the waist. The wetted rib is drawn slowly over the hot iron. Do not force the bending, but feel the wood 'relax' into the required shape as it is drawn over the iron. You can easily crack the wood by using too much pressure, so take your time and increase the curvature gradually.

10 Check frequently whether the rib fits the former; trial and error is the only way to do this. As each section is bent it may be helpful to clamp it to the former and allow it to cool.

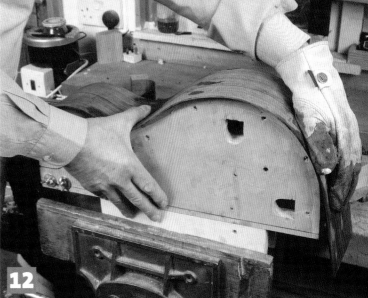

11 When you judge that the shape of the waist is satisfactory – that is, when it can be fitted to the former without difficulty – move on to the upper and lower bouts in turn.

12 It is normal for the wood to need a little persuasion when fitting it to the mould, but it should not have to be wrestled into place by brute force. If it will only fit with great difficulty, then you have more bending to do.

13 Once the shape is nearly right, a little patient adjustment on the bending iron will make all the difference.

14 When you are satisfied that the shape of the bent rib conforms to that of the former, clamp the rib to the former using as many clamping blocks as necessary. Once it has cooled and dried, it will retain its shape when removed from the former, give or take a little spring-back.

LININGS

Linings come in two basic forms: either a solid, continuous strip bent in the same manner as the ribs, or a kerfed strip which can be bent without heat; both of these can be attached to the rib prior to its being glued to the soundboard. There is little difference in strength, but the continuous strip looks better on the completed guitar – though most of it will be unseen, except to the repairer many years hence. A variation on the kerfed strip is the traditional single pieces called *peones* (pawns) by Spanish makers, which need to be added after the rib has been glued to the soundboard.

15 When the first rib has been bent and clamped on the former, you can then bend one of the linings and clamp it to the cooling rib. The lining needs to be no thicker than ⁵⁄₃₂in (4mm); if it is any thicker it will not bend smoothly and you will get hard spots that will not make contact with the rib.

16 When both rib and lining have cooled and set, the rib can continue to be held on the former while the lining is glued to the soundboard edge of the rib. This helps to preserve the shape of the rib. Clamp using either proprietary spring clamps or clothes pegs (clothespins) reinforced with rubber bands.

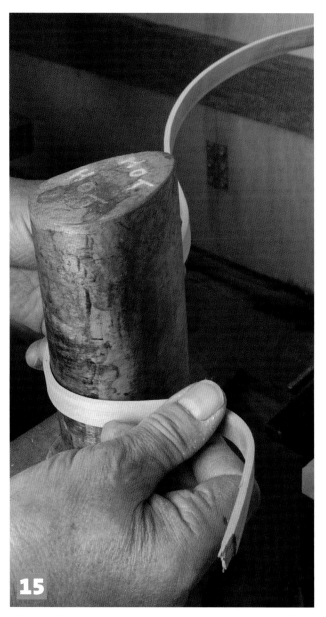

15

16

17 When the glue has dried and set, remove the rib assembly and complete the other rib in the same way. The sharp curves of the cutaway area need extra care, but by this stage you should be feeling reasonably confident.

18 Once the rib, complete with lining, has been unclamped from the former, the gluing edge needs to be planed to provide a good fit to the soundboard. Then sand the inside face of the rib, making sure you remove all the marks left by the bending process. Work down to 400-grit paper to get a nice smooth finish on the rosewood. The final task is to pare the inside edge of the lining to the profile shown inset. Again, sand smooth and polish with 400-grit wet and dry.

5 THE BACK

The finished back, in elaborately figured and carefully bookmatched Brazilian rosewood

The back plates are normally supplied sanded to about ¼in (6mm). Some suppliers will reduce them to the thickness you require, thus saving you a lot of time in scraping and sanding them. Depending on the wood selected, they need to be about ³⁄₁₆in (4.5–5mm) before assembly; note that the back will not be reduced to its final thickness until after the two plates have been glued together.

JOINTING THE BACK

1 Lay the two halves of the back side by side on the bench and adjust their positions, trying to line up the reflecting patterns in the grain. Be aware, before you mark and cut the centre joint, that you will need to trim equal amounts from each plate; otherwise the patterns might shift, and you will lose the mirror effect so much admired in fine guitars.

MATERIALS

- Bookmatched rosewood guitar back, each half 20 x 8 x ¼in (510 x 200 x 6mm)
- Mahogany or spruce for 4 braces, ³⁄₄ x ¼in (19 x 6mm), longest 15½in (395mm)
- Cross-grained mahogany or spruce for back seam support, ³⁄₄ x ³⁄₁₆in (19 x 5mm), to make up to 15½in (395mm) length

PLAIN OR FANCY?

Some makers of extremely fine guitars join the back with no inlay on the centre seam, wishing to show the figure of the wood in its full glory. Others inlay a contrasting piece of suitable timber down the centre seam – usually to match the binding used on the edges of the body – which normally carries up the end of the body at the junction between the ribs.

If the wood you or your customer have chosen is not quite wide enough, a straight or tapered piece of contrasting wood can be inserted to widen it. If only a small amount is required, a nondescript piece of wood, called a spreader strip, can be used and subsequently concealed by the inlay.

The finely figured wood chosen for this instrument needs no extra decoration, which would only detract from the symmetrical effect of the bookmatching.

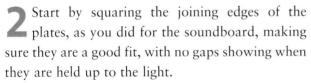

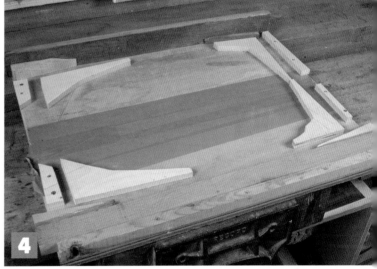

2 Start by squaring the joining edges of the plates, as you did for the soundboard, making sure they are a good fit, with no gaps showing when they are held up to the light.

3 A home-made right-angled sanding block is sometimes a useful aid when refining the joint.

4 A workboard fitted with fences and wedges, all made from offcuts of plywood, is an effective way of clamping the plates together. Parcel tape prevents the back from sticking to the workboard.

5 Once the joint is tight and the bookmatching gives the desired effect, assemble the back plates on the workboard and glue them together. The oil content of rosewood sometimes makes gluing difficult, so an epoxy adhesive may be the best option. Remember that the inside of the guitar back will have a crossbanded strip glued to it to reinforce the joint.

6 & 7 The wedges are gently driven home and the back weighted to keep it flat.

8 When dry, the glue line is scraped clean with a razor blade. Now look carefully once more at both sides of the back and choose which will be the outside face. Place the back plate on the workboard with the inside face down, and sand or scrape the surface till it is flat, then turn it over and sand or scrape it down to the desired thickness, using small clamps to grip the work by its edge.

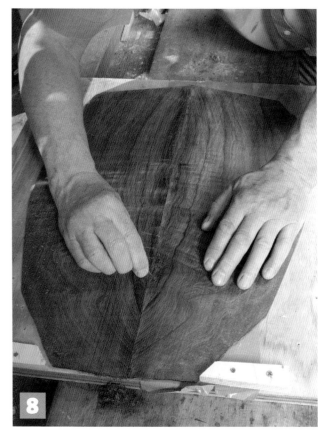

TIP

When sanding bookmatched timber –
especially when it has heavily figured grain –
watch for changes in the grain pattern as the
wood gets thinner. This is due to the grain of
this type of wood not being perfectly vertical.

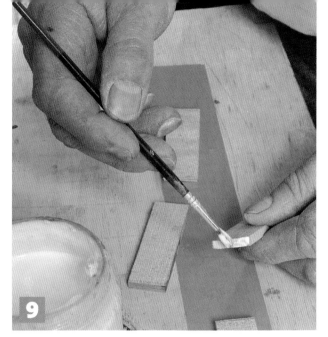

BACK SEAM REINFORCEMENT

9 Before you cut out the outline of the back, the back seam needs to be strengthened with a strip of cross-grained timber down its length. This is made by gluing together offcuts, around ¾ x ³⁄₁₆in (20 x 5mm) in section, to make up the required length. Some makers use spruce, but it is normally made from offcuts of mahogany left over from making the neck. It needs to fill the space between the neck block and the bottom block, but it does no harm to make it longer at this stage.

10 The strip is glued in place and clamped in the go-bar frame.

11 When set, the edges of the reinforcing strip can be neatly rounded. Do not feather the edges; leave a step of about ¹⁄₃₂in (1mm).

SHAPING THE BACK

12 Take the template for the guitar body shape and mark the outline of the back just as you did for the soundboard. As before, use a small washer to draw a second line about ¼in (6mm) outside the first; this is the line to which the back plate will be cut. The outline can now be cut out in the same way as the soundboard. If the blade of your coping saw tends to jam, gently rubbing it with candle wax will help it to slide more freely.

BACK BRACES

13 Referring to the plans, prepare the timber to size for the back braces. You can use spruce or dark mahogany. They are made from 1 x ¼in (25 x 6mm) strips of vertical-grained timber, long enough to span the width of their relevant positions on the back. The mahogany I used was recycled, as you can see from its varnished edges. The curvature of the back is created by the radius carved on the back braces. The simplest way to draw this curve is to make a template of the curvature, then transfer it to the back brace for cutting. The waist brace, being shorter, will require a smaller radius than the others.

CURVE TEMPLATES

To set out the template, select a piece of modellers' ⅛in (3mm) plywood long enough to span the back of the guitar plus about 2in (50mm), and about 2in (50mm) wide. Plane one edge straight and mark it in the middle with a vertical line on both faces; also mark at each end where the edge of the back will come. On one side, draw a line parallel to the planed edge and about 1½in (38mm) away from it. To draw the radius, start by inserting small panel pins where the vertical line representing the outside edge of the back intersects the parallel line drawn earlier. On the centre line, draw a mark ³⁄₁₆in (5mm) above the parallel line, and insert a third pin here. Spring a steel ruler between the three pins, and carefully draw a line along the edge of the ruler. (The photo shows this technique being used directly on the brace itself, which is a method you might prefer if you are only making one instrument and do not wish to make a template.) The pencilled divisions on my template are not essential.

Using a ruler and panel pins to draw a smooth, fair curve

14 Plane down to this line, finishing with a small sanding block which has a plywood fence glued to its side (illustrated on page 15) to ensure that the narrow strip of timber is square on its edge. Check the curvature by rocking the brace on a flat surface; it should be smooth, with no flat spots. This is what gives the back of the guitar a fair curve across its width.

15 Referring to the plans for placement, mark out the back for the braces. They must all be square to the centre line.

16 Use a fine backsaw and a chisel to cut openings in the crossbanding for the braces to fit snugly into.

17 Glue and cramp the braces onto the back, making sure that they are square to the centreline and that you have pulled the back up to the curve of the brace, and not vice versa. Once again, my preferred method is to use the go-bar frame. This requires the making of a workboard with suitably curved cauls fastened to it at the back brace locations.

18 When the glue has set, the braces can be shaped for fitting to the ribs. Plane a radius on the crown of each brace and scallop the ends down to 5/16in (8mm); masking tape protects the back during this operation.

6 ASSEMBLY

Up to now we have been building the main components or subassemblies of the guitar; now is the time to start putting them together. By the end of this chapter we will have a recognizable instrument, though there is still plenty to do before it can be played.

MATERIALS

All the components made so far, plus:
- Willow for linings: 2 pieces 36 x $^3/_4$ x $^5/_{32}$in (915 x 19 x 4mm)

TIP

Assembling the guitar may seem a complex operation, but we will tackle it in manageable stages. The most important thing is to carry out a dry run of every step, so you know what goes where and have all clamps and cauls adjusted and ready to hand before you reach for the glue pot.

PREPARATION

1 Before the neck can be attached to the soundboard, the neck block must be notched to accommodate the ends of the A-braces. Lay the end of the neck over the completed soundboard and mark where the ends of the A-braces will enter.

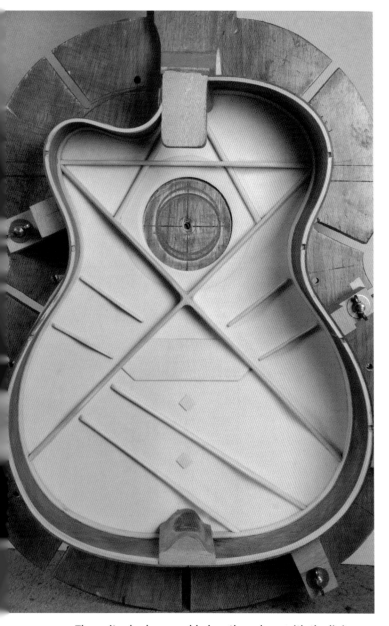

The guitar body assembled on the solera, with the linings notched to receive the back

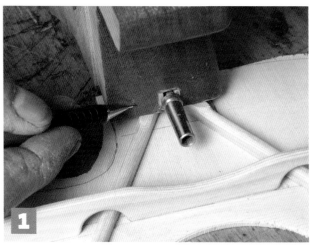

2 Transfer these marks to the top surface of the neck using a sliding bevel, and use a fine backsaw and a chisel to cut the sockets for the ends of the braces. If the braces need shortening a little to avoid fouling the truss rod, do this with a fine backsaw, being careful not to cut into the soundboard in the process.

3 The bass rib must be cut at an angle to fit the angled slot in the neck block. Self-adhesive paper labels make the pencil marks show up clearly. Clamp the rib to the solera and mark accurately where the centre line of the body will come. Mark this position with a try square; you can then measure from the neck itself how much material needs to be cut away so that the rib will fit into the full depth of the slot.

4 The rib on the cutaway side is clamped to the solera and a square is used to mark the cut line exactly at right angles to the soundboard plane. Both the marked ends can now be cut with a fine backsaw. The bottom ends of the ribs are left overlong at this stage.

SOUNDBOARD, NECK AND ENDBLOCK

5 Before refitting the soundboard to the solera, wipe the surface clean; any dust or shavings can mark the surface of the soundboard, and you will not see it again till after the back has been added. Position the soundboard on the centre line, checking the alignment carefully at both ends. Place small pieces of polythene under the areas where the neck and endblock will be attached, to prevent any glue squeeze-out sticking the soundboard to the solera. Fit the threaded rods at either side of the neck-block and endblock positions, and attach a few of your L-shaped clamping blocks to hold the soundboard firmly in place. Before you apply any glue, go through the procedure of assembling the neck, endblock and cauls to make sure everything fits. Also reclamp both ribs to the soundboard and check the fit; then remove them and lay them safely aside.

Apply glue to the neck and place it on the soundboard, fit the caul and wing nuts, and tighten just enough to keep it in place. Check and double-check that the centre line of the neck matches the centre line of the solera, then clamp the neck firmly to the solera and tighten the wing nuts. Clean up any excess glue before it dries.

NECK ANGLE

The guitar shown in the plans has its neck set back by $5/32$in (4mm) at the nut position; hence the spacer inserted between the neck and the solera, which can be seen in photo 5. Setting back the neck increases the string-break angle at the bridge, giving a more bell-like sound and helping to obtain a low action.

6 To ensure that the endblock is at 90° to the soundboard, fit one of your 90° clamping blocks behind it. Remember that the endblock must align with the *inside* face of the ribs, so it must be set in from the external body outline by an amount equal to the thickness of the ribs. Apply glue to the base and position the endblock against the clamping block. Fit the clamping caul and tighten the wing nuts. Temporarily remove the clamping block so you can use a square (resting on a small piece of wood so as to clear the edge of the soundboard) to check that the endblock is upright; adjust if necessary, then replace the clamping block. When the glue has set, clamp the endblock to the clamping block and remove the cauls.

FITTING THE RIBS

7 Screw a temporary stabilizing brace between the endblock and the neck; this will support the endblock during the fitting of the ribs.

Do a dry fit of the ribs and make any necessary adjustments, especially where the bass-side rib fits into its slot. Sometimes, when fitting the neck to the soundboard, some glue will get into the bottom of the slot, preventing the rib from seating properly. If necessary, clean the slot with a folded piece of 80-grit sandpaper, then lightly sand the inside face of the rib. The end of the lining will need to be trimmed off flush with the outside of the heel; use a fine backsaw and take care not to cut into the rib.

The contact area between ribs, linings and soundboard needs to be a good fit, for both mechanical and acoustic purposes. The joint is basically a hinge for the vibration of the soundboard, and needs to be strong and flexible.

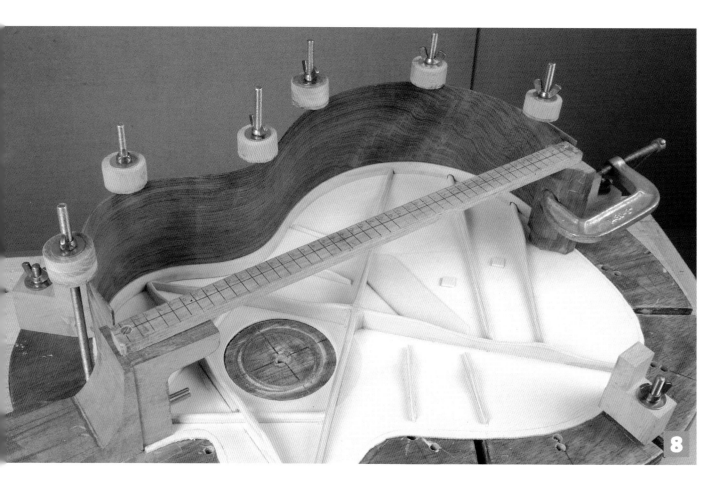

8 To fit the ribs, start by trimming the ends of all the braces to ⁵⁄₆₄in (2mm) inside the outline of the guitar, parallel to the outline drawn on the soundboard. Fit the remaining clamping blocks to

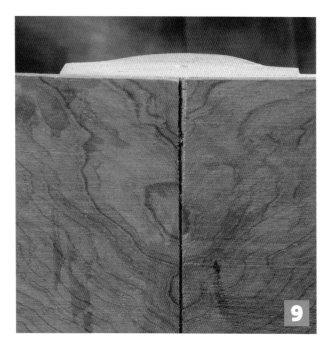

the solera. Place one of the ribs on the soundboard and lightly clamp it to the clamping blocks. Make sure the *outside* face of the rib follows the marked outline of the body. Carefully mark the soundboard brace positions onto the linings, then remove the rib and, using a fine backsaw and chisel, cut the notches for the braces to fit into, being careful you don't cut into the ribs.

After the linings have been notched, refit the rib to the soundboard. Check that it now fits snugly down onto the soundboard with no gaps; readjust if necessary.

9 Only when it is properly fitted and clamped in position can the bottom end of the rib be marked and cut to shape, so as to end as accurately as possible on the centre line of the endblock. The end of the lining will need to be cut back where it meets the endblock. The joint between the two ribs does not need to be perfect, because is it normally covered with a decorative infill strip.

10 When you have determined that both ribs fit the soundboard, neck and endblock, you are ready to glue the ribs to the soundboard. Assemble all the solera clamping blocks, spool clamps, your chosen glue and any other bits that you will be using; for a cutaway model, you will need a G-cramp (C-clamp) and plywood caul to secure the end of the cutaway rib to the side of the neck block. Apply a thin bead of glue to the gluing surface of the rib and lining, making sure that you get glue into the sockets in the linings where the braces will fit, and a liberal amount on the ends of the ribs where they fit into the neck. Fit the ribs to the soundboard and clean up the squeezed-out glue. Be careful when cleaning inside the body, and try not to stain the soundboard with glue.

When the glue has set you can remove the temporary brace, but it is useful to keep the clamping blocks in place till you are ready to attach the back.

11 Looking at the side elevation of the guitar on the plans, you will notice that the back of the body arches from the waist forward to the neck, and also from just aft of the lower bout down to the end of the body. To achieve this arching it will be necessary to remove material from the ribs before you fit the linings.

First apply some white parcel labels to the edge of the rib, as before, to enable you to see your pencil line against the figure of the wood. Measure vertically down the edge of the rib at the neck and mark the dimension given on the plans. Using a spring cramp, fasten a piece of stiff card to the rib

and wrap it around to the centre of the waist; you will need to clamp it to the rib where the curve reverses at the waist. Trace this line on the rib between the neck and the waist. Repeat this process at the bottom end of the body, and on the other side. You can now plane the ribs down to just above this line. Do not reduce the height of the heel or end blocks at this stage.

Prepare and bend the linings for the back edge of the ribs, just as you did for those on the soundboard side, and fit them dry to the ribs. It is easiest if the linings are clamped at the waist while the ends are worked and fitted independently. At the cutaway, the end of the lining needs to be tapered to fit between the rib and the neck. When the linings are ready, glue them to the ribs, cleaning up any excess that squeezes out. After the glue has set, shape and sand these linings to the same profile as the top linings. Then plane the linings down to the ribs and on down to the line drawn earlier on the rib, before removing the paper labels.

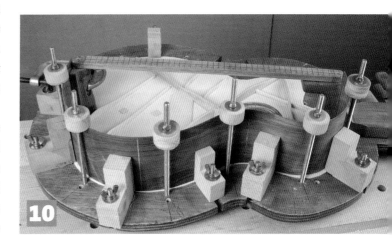

12 If the back of the guitar has a steep arch, you may find that the heel block is too low; in this case, just build up the 'slipper' part of the heel with a spare piece of neck wood, reprofile to match the heel and seal with sanding sealer.

13 The slipper and the endblock now need to be shaped to a curved profile both across the guitar and lengthwise, to fit the back. One way to achieve this is to use a sanding paddle to sand the neck block and rib at the same time. Check your progress by taking a steel ruler and springing it over the slipper block; you should see a fair curve on the ruler when looked at from the front of the guitar. The arch at the end of the slipper block should be the same as that in the upper-bout back brace, which will sit just in front of the neck block in the completed guitar. Gradually decrease the radius on the slipper as you approach the front.

FITTING THE BACK

14 Lay the back on top of the body, making sure that the centre line of the back aligns with the centre line of the soundboard and the middle of the heel. If this is not done accurately, the end inlay strip will not be vertical and the guitar will not look symmetrical. Mark the linings where the back braces touch; also mark the braces at the outside edge of the ribs.

15 Remove the back and transfer the marks made on the ribs across and down the side of the linings. Measure the depth of each back brace at the place where it touched the rib, and transfer this measurement to the lining. Using a small, fine-tooth saw, cut the edges of the brace slot into the linings. If the braces are square on top, then a chisel will suffice for removing the waste material, but if you have radiused the top edges of the braces a small-radius gouge will be better – especially in the area of the waist, where the joints will be visible through the soundhole on the completed guitar.

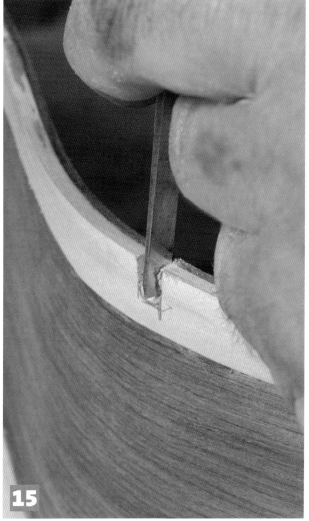

TIP

To hold the back in position, use short lengths of masking tape – but don't use this on the soundboard, as it will tear the grain of the softwood.

16 Trim the ends of the braces, subtracting the thickness of the ribs from the pencil mark you have already made.

17 Now try fitting the back. You may have to make some adjustments till the ribs fit down into the notches in the linings. The back-seam reinforcing strip may also have to be shortened to clear the endblock and slipper block. When satisfied that the back fits well, put it aside for a moment.

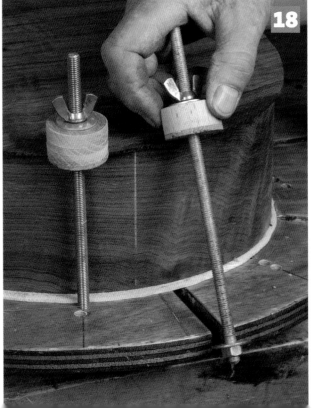

18 The solera now needs to be prepared for the gluing of the back. Remove most of the clamping blocks, though you may prefer to keep one at the end and one each side of the lower bout; the special clamps for the neck and endblock will also be needed. Screw the threaded rods into the tapped holes in the solera, and prepare all your spool clamps. Now remove the inspection plate from the solera (see page 45 step 8), being careful not to knock the guitar out of alignment.

19 Apply a fine bead of glue to the rib/lining surface and into the back-brace sockets, then carefully fit the back to the guitar. Fit the neck caul, and add the bobbins, washers and wing nuts to the threaded rods. Tighten the wing nuts till the glue starts to ooze out. Remove the remaining clamping blocks and fit the spool clamps into the slots where the clamping blocks normally fit. Work around the body, gently tightening all the wing nuts. Excess glue squeeze-out on the inside needs to be cleaned before it sets. This can be done by turning the whole assembly over and working through the inspection hole, using a long-handled artist's paintbrush and a damp cloth.

Now for the moment you have been waiting for: the glue has set, and it is time to remove the guitar from the solera. It looks a little odd at this stage; the neck, which is still full width, gives a false perspective of the final shape. Don't worry: when the neck is carved, the ugly duckling emerges into an elegant swan.

20&21 After you have removed the guitar from the solera, trim off the overhanging edges of the back and soundboard and sand the edges square ready for purfling and binding. The purfling inlay gives the guitar body its decoration, and the binding covers the end grain of the soundboard and back.

99

7 PURFLING AND BINDING

The bindings in place, showing a variation on the traditional clamping method

The bindings around the edge of the body protect the end grain of the soundboard and back from damage, and also help to set off the lines of the guitar. The purfling, which runs around the body of the instrument next to the binding, is for decoration only.

You can purchase pre-made purfling and bindings in either plastic or wood from luthier suppliers, who will list many colour and wood combinations in their catalogues. Purfling and binding are normally available in strips about 36in (915mm) long. Alternatively, you can make your own. Ready-made binding strips usually have a strip of purfling glued to the base. This helps when it comes to bending the purfling to the body contour, as the purfling bends at the same time as the binding, without deforming.

MATERIALS

- 10 strips of triple-veneer purfling, 36in (915mm) long; also contrasting veneer strips as desired
- 4 strips of ebony or other hardwood of your choice, ³⁄₈ x 2 x 36in (10 x 51 x 915mm)

MAKING PURFLING AND BINDINGS

The simplest purfling can be made from three strips of veneer. Normally the colour make-up is black–white–black or white–black–white. Just glue the three chosen strips together – don't be too generous with the glue – and when the glue has set cut them into strips ³⁄₁₆in (5mm) wide. The bindings normally consist of a strip of purfling with a ³⁄₁₆ x ³⁄₈in (5 x 10mm) strip of hardwood glued to the top.

It is a relatively easy job to make your own bindings. Take three strips of 0.02 or 0.012in (0.5 or 0.3mm) veneer, 2in (50mm) wide by 36in (915mm) long, and a strip of hardwood of your choice, ⅜ x 2 x 36in (10 x 50 x 915mm), and glue them together. A simple way to do the gluing is to stick a couple of strips of 2in (50mm) plastic parcel tape to the bench, apply the glue to the layers of veneer, then put the hardwood strip on top; I use cork-faced lead weights to hold them down till the glue sets. When the glue has set, clean the edges and saw the sandwich up into strips ³⁄₁₆in (5mm) wide. To save wastage, I use the small 12-volt bench-top tablesaw shown on page 17, with a 2in (50mm) diameter narrow-kerfed blade fitted. When sawing single layers of veneer, I use a small hold-down just to the rear of the blade to prevent the friction of the blade from lifting the sawn veneer up and damaging it.

DESIGN CONSIDERATIONS

1 For our guitar we will use a fairly standard system of body decoration. This consists of triple-veneer purfling and bindings for the back and sides, while the

front has a double line of purfling with contrasting strips sandwiched in between, in keeping with the soundhole inlay. The binding and purfling are inlaid in stages, but photo 1 shows, for demonstration's sake, how the complete set for the front would look if it were made up in one piece. The back of a guitar is normally less ornate than the soundboard; some makers even omit the purfling altogether and just fit a single piece of binding.

2 The purfling and binding are glued into small L-shaped rebates cut out of the edge of the guitar body. The rebates can be cut by hand using a violin maker's purfling cutter and a chisel, or with a small trimming router fitted with a suitable base, as we did for the soundhole inlay. The rebate is cut in two stages: first the horizontal portion to take the purfling – which in our case must be made wider on the soundboard than on the back – then the vertical portion to take the binding.

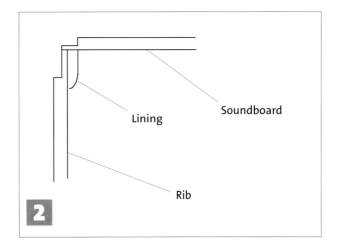

2 Lining — Soundboard — Rib

END-SEAM INLAY

3 The first part of the inlay sequence is the end-seam strip – the inlay over the joint where the ribs meet at the bottom end. Start by gently gripping the guitar in the bench vice by the neck, with the endblock facing up. Identify the centre line of the soundboard and transfer it over the end of the guitar, then do the same with the back. Both lines should coincide – if not, you will have to decide whether to line up the inlay with the soundboard or the back.

TIP

Although a parallel-sided inlay strip is shown here, a wedge-shaped strip will alleviate any problem of misalignment, as well as being easier to fit.

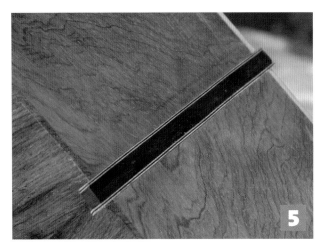

4 Start by taking a short section of binding material and gluing strips of purfling to both edges. When the glue has set, scrape both faces flat. Lay the strip on the back in the centre and mark the width of the strip on the end of the body, using a sharp marking knife. Carefully cut down both lines with a fine-toothed saw, and with a sharp chisel remove the wood from between the lines.

5 The inlay should go in to the full thickness of the ribs; it should be a snug fit, and stand proud of the ribs by just a whisker so that it can be cleaned down flush afterwards.

Remove the inlay and set it aside until the purfling and binding rebates have been cut. If you are going to machine the rebates, you will need to dry-fit a temporary end-seam strip, sanded flush with the ribs, to prevent the router's follower wheel dropping into the end-strip groove and causing the cutter to cut too deep into the back or soundboard. (Don't use the real end-seam strip for this – its ends could easily get trimmed off short by mistake.)

CUTTING THE REBATES

6 Clamp the guitar in a high-level vice or similar. Measure the width of the bindings and purfling to determine how far in to set your cutter. Since our guitar does not have a back-seam inlay, we can start the purfling rebate at the neck (or as close to the neck as the router base will allow) and work our way around the periphery of the guitar. If you have inlaid the back joint, the binding rebate will need to stop short of the back seam to allow for the mitre on the back-seam inlay strip, which is cut by hand with a chisel.

When you have completed the purfling rebates on the back and soundboard, repeat the same operation on the ribs for the bindings. If you are using a router, don't try to cut the binding rebates in one pass – take several cuts.

ROUTING THE REBATES

My favourite tool for rebating is a small router fitted with a purpose-made base from a specialist luthiers' supplier. One drawback with a power cutter is that the slight curvature of both soundboard and back may cause the trimmer to tilt, giving inaccurate depth and width to the rebate. Working slowly and patiently, cutting in very small increments, will help. If you opt to use a hand-held purfling cutter and chisel instead, any variations in curvature of the front or back can be compensated for during the chiselling; a very sharp chisel and extreme patience are required for this delicate operation.

The router needs to be fitted with a very sharp carbide cutter. Be particularly careful when cutting the waist area on both the front and the back, as the cutter will be cutting into the grain and can cause it to tear out. Extra care is also needed for the soundboard, because spruce, cedar and redwood are very soft timbers with alternating hard and soft grain, and unless you are very careful you will produce a ragged edge which is almost impossible to eradicate.

Binding and purfling rebates can be cut on a spindle moulder with an appropriate stepped cutter, but this is outside the scope of this book.

The miniature router set up for working the rebates

7 At the corner where the body meets the neck, only hand methods can be used. Score across with a scalpel and straightedge, then use a narrow, very sharp chisel to remove the waste. The end of the purfling will be concealed under the fretboard.

8 & 9 The photographs of the guitar back show the more laborious hand method of rebating. First the purfling cutter is used to score the edge of the rebate, then the waste is carefully removed with a sharp chisel. Particular care is needed in the waist area, which must be approached from both directions, paying attention to any sudden changes in grain direction.

10 A home-made sanding block with integral fence can be a useful tool for ensuring that the rebate is square.

11 The short section at the heel is cut by hand with a sharp knife or scalpel. Note the narrow recess between the heel and the cutaway rib, which will be filled with a strip of purfling.

FITTING THE PURFLING

12 Assemble the stack of veneers for the purfling and drop a spot of superglue (cyanoacrylate) onto the end of the stack, being careful not to glue your fingers to the veneers. When dry, trim the end with a chisel or scalpel at 45°, leaving just enough of the glued portion as is necessary to hold the stack together.

13 Starting at the centre seam, apply glue to the rebate and carefully work your way around the periphery of the body, holding the purfling in place with pins or short lengths of tape. Hide glue is best for this operation, as it grabs immediately and holds the purfling in place securely as it cools; superglue can stain the wood. Work carefully around the body, making sure that the purfling seats properly in the waist area.

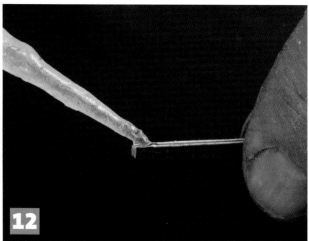

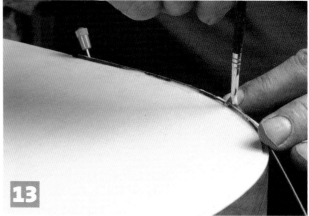

14 Clip off the end so it fits into the hand-cut rebate at the neck joint.

FITTING THE BINDINGS

15 Trim the permanent end-seam infill strip on one end at 90°, then carefully trim the purfling on either side of it at 45°, using the reflection in the chisel as a guide (see page 62 step 9). Now remove the temporary end-seam strip and glue the permanent one in place. The mitred end of the purfling on the infill strip will meet up with the purfling on the bindings, when installed; the photo shows the binding complete on one side, so you can see how the finished joint should look. The other end of the end-seam inlay will be trimmed to length when the back bindings are fitted.

16 The rebates need to be scraped clean of glue before the bindings are fitted. The bindings must be pre-bent, in the same way as the linings; otherwise they are liable to break when being fitted. Once again, hide glue is a good choice.

Dry-fit the bindings first, starting at the end of the body. Mitre the purfling so that it fits the end-seam strip as shown in the previous photo; note that the binding proper must extend beyond the mitre so as to meet in a butt joint on the centre line of the guitar. Work your way around the body till you get to the neck, where the bindings are butt-jointed on a symmetrical instrument, or mitred (as seen in photo 18) on a cutaway model. On the soundboard they are let into the sockets cut into the neck, which will be hidden underneath the fretboard when fitted. Glue them on one at a time, starting from the end mitre.

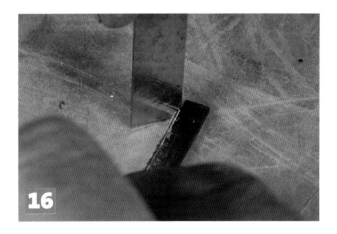

TIP

Be careful when scraping inlay veneers, as they can tear and leave small divots that trap dark sawdust.

17 In place of the traditional string to clamp the bindings in place, I now use rubber strapping made from garden pond liner cut into strips ½in (13mm) wide. Wind it as closely as necessary to hold the bindings securely in position.

18&19 Finally, the exposed end of the heel is pared back to the depth of the binding and fitted with a matching cap.

When complete, sand and scrape the bindings and purfling smooth. Remember when sanding that dark wood such as rosewood will stain lighter-coloured woods, especially spruce. I usually finish by applying a coat of sanding sealer to the white purfling strips and the soundboard to keep them clean while working on the other parts.

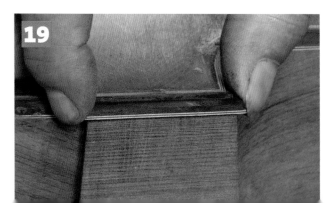

HEAD BINDINGS

Binding the edge of the head is an optional feature, and you may skip this section if you wish. The simpler alternative of fitting multiple head veneers, giving a striped pattern at the edges, was described on page 55, step 26.

20 The veneers for the binding are chosen to complement those of the body and fretboard. They must be pre-bent to the profile of the head, but, because they are short, they are a little awkward to handle on the bending iron. A flexible metal strap held behind the binding helps with this.

21 For this instrument, a strip of white–black–white purfling was applied first, followed by the same edge binding that was used on the body. The corners of the purfling need to be mitred for continuity, but the outer binding at the sides can be allowed to overlap as shown, and trimmed back later.

22 The same design will be used on the fretboard (see next chapter), to give a unified appearance to the whole instrument.

23 A purfling inlay on the soundboard around the end of the fretboard is an optional extra that I like to include on some of my guitars.

8 THE FRETBOARD

If the soundboard is the equivalent of the engine in a car, then the fretboard is the equivalent of the engine management system. They have to work perfectly together to produce the ultimate performance, so accuracy in making and fitting is vital. Fretboards can be made from any tight-grained hardwood, from oak to rosewood. Most guitars use one of three woods: ebony, maple or one of the rosewood family.

MATERIALS

- Ebony or rosewood, 17½ x 2½ x ¼in (445 x 65 x 6mm)
- 38in (960mm) of purfling and binding material to match guitar body (optional)
- Bone for top nut, 2 x ½ x ¼in (50 x 13 x 6mm)
- Position markers as desired
- Fret wire, about 4½ft (1.37m)

Dressing the ends of the frets

MAKING THE FRETBOARD

1 Start by planing the fretboard flat and to a thickness of ¼in (6mm). Plane one of the edges square and straight for reference.

2 Decide which side is to be the fret face and carefully draw a centre line on this face, parallel to the reference edge. Draw a square line across the fretboard at the top nut end; this will be the datum from which you measure the fret positions. Repeat this for the 12th fret position, which will be equal to half the scale length measured from the top nut. Taking the dimensions from the plan, measure the fretboard width at the top nut – normally about 1¾in (44mm) – and divide this by two. Measure this distance out from the centre line on each side, and mark it on the nut line. Now measure the width at the 12th fret and mark this in the same way. Join up these marks and extend the lines to both ends of the fretboard blank. This shows the taper you need to create. It is important to get this correct, as the fretboard becomes the template for the neck taper when you do the final shaping of the neck. For the sake of clarity, the lines in the photo have been drawn in white pencil.

Marking the fret positions across the fretboard is done using a square and a sharp pencil; alternatively, you can paint the surface of the fretboard with diluted white poster paint and use a square and an engineer's scribe to mark the fret positions.

TIP

If the fretboard is already tapered when you buy it, it is worth gluing a wedge-shaped piece to one edge to provide a square reference face when marking out the fret positions.

FINDING THE FRET POSITIONS

To calculate the fret positions on the fretboard, use the following method:

Divide the scale length of the guitar by 17.81715; this is the distance from the nut to the first fret. Subtract this figure from the scale length and divide the remainder – that is, the distance from the first fret to the datum point at the bridge – again by 17.81715; this is the distance from the first fret to the second. Repeat this operation till you arrive at the last fret. As a check, the 5th fret should fall at exactly ¼ of the scale length, the 7th fret at ⅓, the 12th fret exactly halfway, the 17th at ⅝ and the 19th at ⅔ of the scale length.

A table of fret positions for our guitar can be found on page 141.

3 To cut the fret slots you will require a low-sided mitre box and a saw with a kerf equal in width to the tang of the fret (the tang is the part of the fret that goes into the fretboard). Some specialist suppliers offer a fret-slot saw and mitre box with an adjustable depth gauge so you can repeatedly cut slots to the same depth. Before you cut the slots, measure the depth of the tang. If your saw is equipped with a depth gauge, set it to this measurement plus about 5/64in (2mm). The additional depth will provide sufficient clearance for the tang after the fretboard has been radiused.

4 & 5 When you have finished cutting the slots, cut the fretboard to length and plane the tapers on both edges. When cutting the fretboard at the top nut position, make sure you cut on the *outside* of the marked line; otherwise the fretboard will be slightly short, and this will affect the intonation of the guitar. Make sure that the edges are straight and square to the gluing surface.

If you are intending to add decorative bindings to the edges of your fretboard, you will have to reduce the width of the fretboard proper to allow for these.

BINDING THE FRETBOARD

Edge bindings give a neat finish to the fretboard, but they are an optional extra and you may skip this section if you prefer.

6 The scheme chosen should be consistent with the treatment used on the body of the guitar; for the instrument shown, I used one row of white–black–white purfling, with a single layer of black binding outside. The purfling strips are glued together on a flat surface and pressed with a roller to ensure good adhesion.

7 The purflings are fitted first, and the fret slots are recut through the purfling; if this were not done, the ends of the frets would have insufficient support.

8 The ends of the purfling are mitred by eye (because the fretboard tapers, the corners are fractionally less than 90°), using the reflection in the chisel as a guide, as before. Lastly, the edge binding is attached, to cover the ends of the fret slots.

TIP

Use double-sided tape to secure the fretboard, bridge blank and other small pieces of work to the bench.

RADIUSING THE SURFACE

9 Fretboard surfaces are usually flat on classical guitars, but slightly convex on steel-strung instruments. The radius is more of a player preference than a fixed design function; it can vary from 7in (178mm) to 18in (457mm) or more, and templates and sanding blocks with these curvatures are available from luthier suppliers.

10 Draw a fat white pencilled centre line down the middle of the fretboard; this serves as a visual reference when planing and sanding. Start the process by taking four or five very thin shavings off both edges of the fretboard, keeping an eye on the centre line. Then change to the radiused sanding block with 80-grit paper. Work up and down the length of the fretboard, watching both edges to make sure you don't work one edge more than the other; remember to keep an eye on the centre line.

11 You can tell you are nearly down to size when the sandpaper starts to rub the pencil line away. When the pencil line starts to show signs of wear, change to finer sandpaper, ending with 400-grit. Check the fretboard for flatness and straightness along its length, as any bumps or hollows will cause an irregular playing surface, resulting in string buzz on adjacent frets.

The fret slots will by now be filled with impacted dust. Carefully remove this and, using a depth gauge, measure the depth of the slots at the outer edge; they may need to be recut a little deeper to ensure enough clearance for the fret tangs. Do not fit the frets yet.

WHEN TO FIT THE FRETS

One reason for not fitting the frets at this stage is that the pressure of the frets in their slots can cause the fretboard to take on a backward bow, thus making it difficult to glue to the neck; the flexing of the fretboard would also make the frets less tight in their slots, making them difficult to seat properly. Another reason is that on steel-strung guitars it is common to inlay fret-position markers into the surface, and on the edge of the fretboard facing the player; these will need to be smoothed and filled after fitting, and the frets would be in the way.

FITTING THE FRETBOARD

12 Check the fit of the fretboard against the neck and soundboard; if the neck on your guitar is angled back, there will be a gap beneath the fretboard at the body end. This can be filled by gluing a thin wedge of neck timber to the underside of the fretboard and carefully paring and scraping this until an exact fit is obtained.

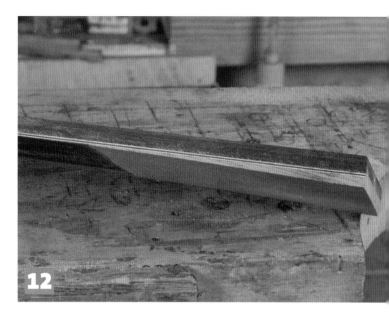

13 Now comes the time to attach the fretboard to the neck. Hold the guitar by the neck in the high-level vice. Redraw the centre line down the length of the fretboard and over the ends. Redraw the fretboard outline, top nut position and centre line on the neck. Place the bone blank for the top nut on the neck against the head veneers, so as to provide a seating position for the fretboard. Line up the centre lines of the fretboard and neck; you will need to temporarily remove the bone nut in order to do this. Lightly clamp the fretboard to the neck, making sure the fretboard is still accurately aligned on the centre line and that the top nut fits snugly against both the fretboard and the head veneers.

14 Take two pieces of scrap hardwood about 8in long by ⅜in square (200 x 10 x 10mm) and cover them completely with plastic packing tape. Place them against each side of the fretboard and, using small screws, fix them to the scrap edges of the neck. These blocks prevent the fretboard from slipping off-centre while being glued.

15 As an additional precaution, take two small panel pins whose diameter is slightly less than the width of the fret slot, cut off their heads, and make a right-angled bend at one end. Drill a hole into the 2nd fret slot – just off centre, so as to miss the truss rod – and another into the 14th fret slot. Carefully tap the pins into the neck through the fretboard, checking the fit of the top nut, then remove the fretboard, with the pins still in it, for gluing. These pins provide for positive positioning and prevent the fretboard from slipping backward when being glued and clamped.

16 Before gluing the fretboard to the neck, assemble all the clamps and cauls and rehearse the process of gluing and clamping the fretboard to the neck. Note the holes drilled in the clamping caul to accommodate the locating pins inserted through the fretboard. Pay especial attention to the caul that goes inside the body under the end of the fretboard; a piece of electricians' insulation tape folded to give a double side of adhesive will help to hold it in place while you position the clamps. Apply low-tack masking tape to the soundboard alongside the fretboard, to prevent glue staining. When you are ready, apply the glue and clamp up. Try not to get glue in the fret slots. When the glue has dried, remove the clamps and cauls, pull out the pins (the bent-over ends make this easier), clean up the excess glue and remove the blocks at the sides of the fretboard.

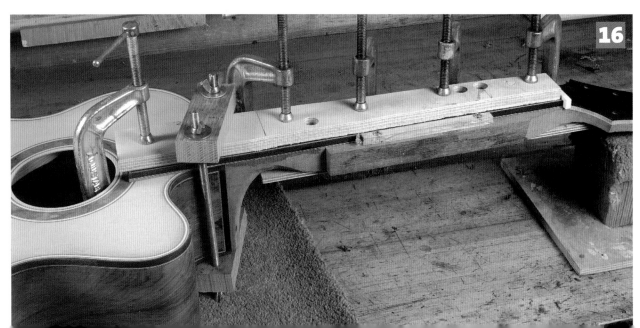

17 Our guitar has position-marker dots on the edge of the fretboard only. These are relatively easy to fit: all that is needed is a brad-point drill equal to the diameter of the dot being inlaid. It is important to use good-quality drills, as cheap ones made from inferior steel are liable to tear the sides of the holes. For side position markers you will need a ⁵⁄₆₄in (2mm) brad-point bit; anything larger than this would look out of proportion to the width of the fretboard edge. Drill the hole just slightly shallower than the thickness of the dot being inlaid, to allow for subsequent trimming. Natural shell can be of different thicknesses, so measure the inlays before drilling the holes.

18 Blow out any dust, and drop a spot of very thin superglue in the hole. Then, using metal tweezers, carefully press the dot into place. You may have to use the side or the handle of the tweezers to seat the dot all the way in. When complete, sand the surface smooth.

TIP

If the wood has torn out at all during drilling, fill the gap with fine sawdust from an offcut of the fretboard, with some superglue dropped on top; when set, sand flush.

FITTING THE FRETS

For this straightforward operation the guitar needs to be supported carefully. If you are working on the bench, make sure you have suitable padding under the body of the guitar – an old blanket folded over or a soft carpet works well – just make sure there are no wood shavings or other debris that could mark the body. The neck will have to be supported as well, especially under the area where you will be hammering in the frets. I prefer to work with the guitar held in the high-level vice, where the neck is securely gripped and the fretboard is up close so it is easier to see what you are doing.

19 Now check one last time that the fretboard is flat along its length. Make any corrections that are necessary, otherwise you will have a lot of extra work levelling the frets after they are fitted.

20 Top-quality fret wire is made from an 18% hard nickel-silver alloy, as described on page 39. The most commonly used size is Dunlop FW6105, whose nominal dimensions are 0.096in (2.438mm) width of crown and 0.047in (1.194mm) tang depth. Fret wire is normally supplied by the foot (305mm), although the shipping cost will be by weight. For our 19-fret guitar you will require around 4½ft (1.37m) of your chosen wire. When you get the wire it will be either in one continuous coil or in sections of a coil. I don't normally straighten it before use, as I find the radius as it comes quite acceptable for my method of fitting.

Start by cutting the frets to about ½in (13mm) longer than the slot length, and place the cut lengths into a holder; this consists of a square block of scrap timber with three rows of holes ⅜in (10mm) deep, numbered in pencil from 1 to 30. This holder helps to keep the cut fret wire from getting lost on the bench, and helps you to fit the correct-length fret to each slot.

TIP

Before you begin, it would be prudent to cover the soundboard to prevent any accidental damage. Masking tape is liable to lift the grain when it is peeled off. A better idea is to take a piece of thick card and cut out the shape of the end of the fretboard and the profile of the body; then you can tape the card to the sides of the guitar. You will need to cut out the soundhole area so you can reach inside when fitting the upper frets. I like to protect the head veneer in the same way.

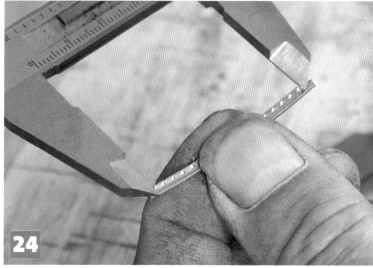

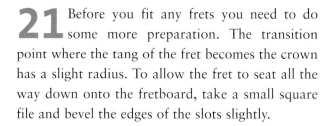

21 Before you fit any frets you need to do some more preparation. The transition point where the tang of the fret becomes the crown has a slight radius. To allow the fret to seat all the way down onto the fretboard, take a small square file and bevel the edges of the slots slightly.

22 Next, clean all the dust out of the fret slots; a scalpel blade with the edge ground off is a useful tool for this purpose.

23 & 24 If your fretboard has edge bindings, the fret slots will be narrower than the overall width of the fretboard. Use the inside legs of your dial callipers to measure each slot, and the outside legs to measure the length of the fret tang.

25 The ends of the tang must then be carefully filed back to fit the slot, leaving enough crown at each end to overlap the binding.

26 I use a small plastic-faced mallet to fit the frets; if you use a metal hammer you run the risk of denting the fret crown, although some luthiers get very good results with a jeweller's wide-faced hammer. Another precaution is to place a mask of slotted metal (see photo 30), once again available from luthier suppliers, on either side of the fret to prevent the plastic face of the mallet denting the fretboard.

I like to start from the top-nut end of the fretboard, and, being right-handed, I have the head of the guitar on my left. This allows me to hold the fret end on the bass side, placing the treble side of the fret into the slot. I tap the fret in starting at the treble end and working across to the bass side.

27 When you get past the 14th fret, the frets will not seat so easily. This is because there is not enough mass behind the fretboard, which

ALTERNATIVE METHODS

Some say that the fret wire should be tapped in at both ends before seating the middle; I tried this once and ended up with a lump in the middle of the fret. I have also tried spring-loaded impact punches fitted with a suitable caul, and pressing with a G-cramp (C-clamp), but none of these methods worked as well as the mallet. If you were in a production-shop environment you would probably want to invest in an arbor press with the correct radiused arbors for pressing in the fret wire.

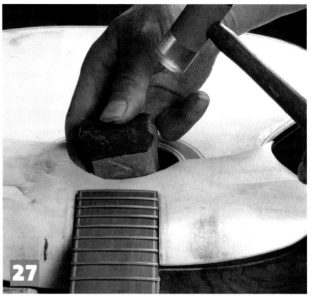

causes the fret wire to bounce. To overcome this I use a small cork-faced lead block held under the fretboard inside the body. This provides the mass needed to hammer against. Start these frets in the usual way, then reach inside with the lead weight and press it against the underside of the soundboard before continuing to seat the fret with the mallet. Be careful of the bracing and the truss-rod end inside the body.

28 When all the frets have been seated, take a large file and carefully file the ends of the frets flush, being very careful not to mar the edge of the fretboard. (Overlong ends can be clipped off first with side-cutting nippers.) Slightly bevel the ends, but do not bevel too far, or when the guitar is played the strings can sometimes roll off over the edge of the fret.

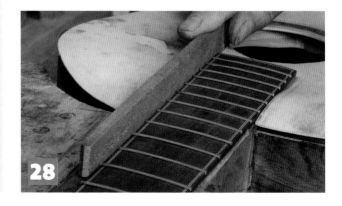

29 After the fret ends have been dressed back to the fretboard and slightly bevelled, it is time to level the tops of the frets. This is where you will be glad you did all that work in preparing the fretboard and getting it straight. I use a diamond-grit stone, holding it at an angle and working in full-length strokes across and along the frets. It will rapidly become obvious where the high spots are. Be careful not to take too much off the tops of the frets, just enough to remove the high spots.

30 Next take a fret-crowning file (a specialist tool with concave edges) and reshape the tops of the frets, using the slotted metal mask mentioned before. They will look quite rough at this stage, but don't worry: when you polish them they will be fine.

31 The last job is to round over the fret ends – what I call 'nosing' the frets. I use a small triangular file with one corner ground and polished flat to form a 'safe' edge. The opposite face I paint white, to prevent me from using the wrong edge. The flat-ground surface slides on the fretboard without leaving more than a slight impression. Rub your hand along the edge: there should be no sharp edges to catch on.

When the nosing is done, replace the metal mask over the fret, then take some 800-grit wet & dry paper and polish the frets. When this is done, use fine steel wool to polish the whole fretboard from end to end; the frets should really shine now. All that is left to do is to wipe the fretboard with some lemon oil, which is especially formulated for fretboards and available in small quantities from luthiers' suppliers.

TIP

On an unbound fretboard, a gap will show below each fret if the tangs do not go all the way to the bottom of their slots; use coloured shellac sticks to fill the holes.

29

30

31

9 SHAPING THE NECK

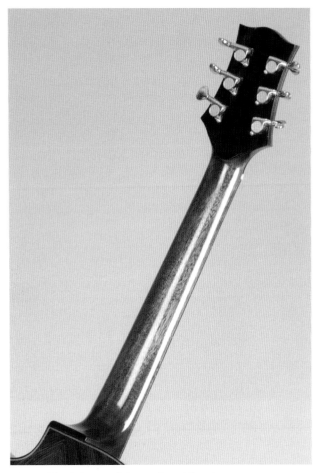

The finished shape of the neck and head

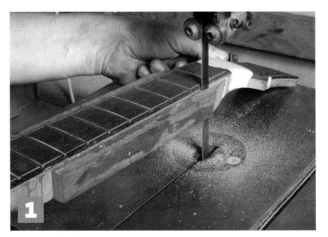

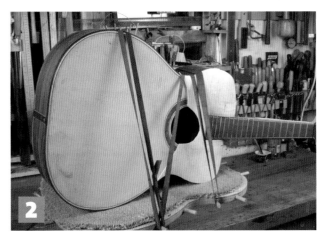

The neck is still oversize at this stage, and must now be brought to its final shape, using the finished fretboard as a guide. The mahogany of the neck is much softer than the ebony fretboard, and it is easier and safer to shape the softer material to the harder than vice versa.

1 Carefully saw off the excess wood on either side of the neck, either on the bandsaw or by hand, leaving just a small margin for planing.

2 The guitar body is now mounted on the workboard shown on page 19, using rubber straps cut from pond-liner material as before. The whole assembly is held in the high-level vice.

3 Plane down the edge of the neck till you reach the edge of the fretboard, being careful not to mar the finished fretboard. Any parts which are inaccessible to the plane will need to be pared with a chisel. Repeat the process on the other side.

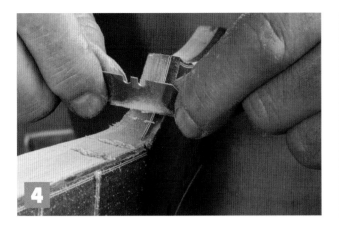

4 The transition area between neck and head is refined by scraping with a utility-knife blade.

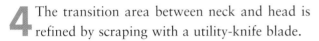

5 Place the guitar face down on the workboard with a piece of carpet or old blanket to protect the face. The neck tapers slightly in thickness, starting from the top nut and slowly increasing in depth towards the heel. To create the taper, start by reducing the area behind the top nut to the finished thickness, then graduate the thickness up to the heel. Stop regularly to check the thickness with callipers, by reference to the full-size plans.

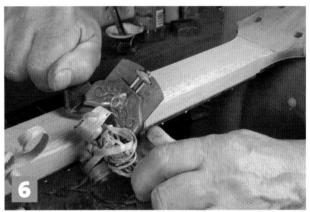

6&7 The cross-section of the neck is D-shaped. The plans show typical sections, but individual makers and players often have their own preferences, so if you have a favourite instrument which is particularly comfortable you may wish to copy that. A concave-faced spokeshave is ideal for this job; a flat-faced shave will also do, but more sanding will be needed to produce a smooth curve. I would not advise using a rasp, as some do. The shaping of the neck should be a tactile exercise, with the neck evolving from a rough rectangular cricket-bat shape to one resembling the elegant wrist of a ballerina.

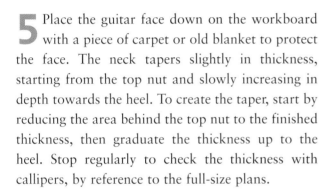

8 Some handwork with a chisel or file will be needed at both ends, especially for rounding off the sweep of the heel. The neck-to-head transition shape will depend on the shape of the neck and on the final head design; refer to the photographs of the finished instrument for guidance.

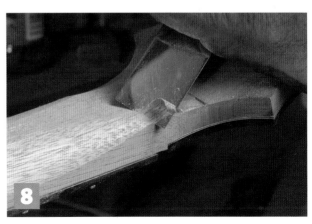

10 THE BRIDGE

The bridge performs two basic functions: to provide an anchoring point for the strings, and to transfer the string vibrations to the soundboard. It is usually made from the same timber as the fretboard. The bridge needs to be light in mass, yet tough enough to stand the tension of the strings pulling on the front edge.

MATERIALS

- Ebony, rosewood or other hard wood, 7 x 1⁷⁄₈ x ⁷⁄₁₆in (178 x 48 x 11mm)
- 6 bridge pins (see page 39)
- Electrical pickup if required

Four stages in shaping the bridge

MAKING THE BRIDGE

1 Bandsaw your bridge blank to the dimensions given above (unless you have bought it already prepared), and inspect it to see if it has any distinguishing marks or grain that you might want to accent.

Start by deciding which face will fit against the soundboard. Plane the underside flat. Using a fret-scale ruler, measure the scale length from the top nut to the saddle position on the soundboard, and place a small mark on the centre line of the soundboard with a soft pencil. Lay a straightedge on the frets at the centre line so that it extends over the saddle position. Carefully measure the distance between the underside of the straightedge and the mark on the soundboard, and reduce the bridge blank to this thickness; it should be in the region of ⅜in (10mm). Plane the front face square and straight to the underside. Cut out the shape of the bridge either on the bandsaw or with a coping saw.

Taking the dimensions from the plans, mark out the shape of the bridge, the positions of the bridge-pin holes and the outline of the saddle slot.

2 The easiest way to shape the scalloped ends of the bridge is on the drum sander.

DESIGN CONSIDERATIONS

If the saddle sits too far forward, or is too shallow, it can, under string tension, split the face of the bridge. In theory, the depth of the saddle slot should never be less than the exposed height of the saddle after the guitar has been set up. A routed depth of ³⁄₁₆in (5mm) should be suitable for most saddles. Consideration also needs to be given to the saddle-slot depth if an under-saddle pickup is to be fitted. Different pickups will enter the saddle slot from different ends. Buy your pickup before making the bridge, and consult the instructions provided by the manufacturer.

TIP

On a small piece of dark wood you may find it difficult to see pencil lines. One solution is to attach self-adhesive paper labels, as we did with the ribs. An alternative is to coat the whole of the face with diluted white poster paint, then use an engineer's sharp metal scriber or similar – I use a small round file sharpened to a point.

3 & 4 The saddle slot can be cut with the small router that was used for the purfling and binding rebates. To do this you will require a simple holding jig, fitted with a small fence to guide the lateral travel of the router. (The fence is the piece at the top in photo 3, secured to the jig with two screws.) The jig is nothing more than a small box, held in the vice, in which the bridge blank sits snugly. It is made from plywood, and the depth of the recess is slightly greater than the overall thickness of the bridge blank. The position of the fence is determined by the size and type of router used. Notice that the saddle slot slopes away from the treble side to the bass side, to compensate for the difference in string diameters; the fence of your jig needs to be fixed precisely parallel to the required slot position.

Some under-saddle pickups require a radius to the bottom of the slot, to ensure 100% contact between the pickup and the saddle; this is easily achieved with a suitable router bit, but cutting this radius by hand would be extremely difficult.

5 When you have completed the saddle slot, drill $\frac{5}{32}$in (4mm) holes for the bridge pins, preferably using a pillar drill for accuracy, and countersink them to provide a ramp for the strings as they exit the pin hole and change direction towards the crown of the saddle. The holes will be reamed to their final dimensions after the bridge has been attached to the soundboard.

6 Use a small hand plane to form a radius on the front and back edges.

7 The final shaping of the bridge is done with sandpaper, with a final buffing on a power polisher, using wax. I don't lacquer my bridges, as over many string changes the lacquer can get scratched and chipped; a wax finish is easily restored by a quick rub with a cloth.

8 The bridge is now almost finished, but the underside needs to be matched to the curvature of the soundboard for maximum adhesion. You can purchase special tools for this operation, but a simple and satisfactory method is to use low-tack tape to stick a piece of 80-grit sandpaper, grit-side up, to the soundboard, and rub the bridge over it in tight figure-of-eight movements till all of the gluing surface has been abraded. Leave the gluing surface of the bridge rough to provide a key for the glue when attaching it to the soundboard.

ANCHORING THE STRINGS

Bridge pins (illustrated on page 39) come in various styles and materials, from fossilized ivory to plastic; there are beautiful turned rosewood ones with mother-of-pearl inlay on the ends. Some pins even have slots carved in the edges for the strings, but this is not necessary for the holding of the strings.

The proper method of anchoring the string is to cut a slot at the front of the bridge-pin hole, equal to the diameter of the wound part of the end of the string. The guitar string is then pressed into this slot and held there by the bridge pin, with the stop on the string trapped against the bridge backing plate underneath; at no time does the bridge pin take the strain of holding against the string tension.

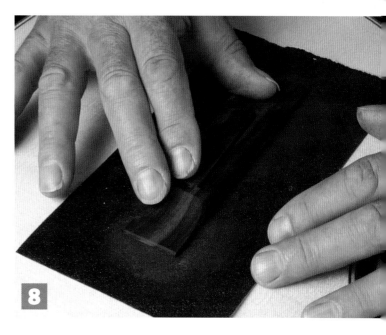

POSITIONING THE BRIDGE

The position of the bridge is critical for the intonation of the guitar, so care must be exercised. We will mark out its definitive location now, but it will not be fitted till after the lacquer has been applied, as the rubbing out and polishing of the lacquer is a lot easier to do without the bridge.

9 Clean off any dust and apply some low-tack masking tape to the soundboard (which is still coated with sanding sealer at this time) in the area of the bridge location.

10 Using a long fret-scale ruler, draw the centre line of the guitar onto the masking tape, then extend the lines of the edges of the fretboard over the tape and draw these two lines, which should be equidistant from the centre line.

The scale length of our guitar is 25½in (648mm), and to compensate for string stretch (see panel) we need to add ⁵⁄₆₄in (2mm) at the first-string position, so the midpoint of the bone saddle where the first string crosses it will be 25³⁷⁄₆₄in (650mm) from the face of the top nut. Use a fret-scale ruler to position the saddle at this distance, making sure the front edge of the bridge is centred and square to the centre line of the fretboard. When satisfied that the bridge is in its correct location, gently clamp it to the soundboard using a long bridge clamp.

SCALE-LENGTH COMPENSATION

A guitar string stretches when it is pressed down onto the fret, and this causes a small but significant rise in pitch. Over the centuries luthiers have attempted to find the best way of compensating for this. A low action minimizes the pitch change; the high actions found on some low-cost imported guitars will need to be lowered to enable the instrument to play in tune. Over time it has been found that an increase of ⁵⁄₆₄in (2mm) in the scale length at the first-string position works well in compensating for this problem.

11 While the bridge is still clamped in position on the soundboard, drill two ¹⁄₁₆in (1.5mm) holes through the saddle slot into the soundboard. These holes will have short hardwood dowels fitted to aid in the relocating of the bridge during the gluing operation.

12 Trace around the bridge with a fine, dark pencil. Then remove the bridge and, using a sharp craft knife, cut out the footprint of the bridge in the masking tape, *just inside* the drawn line. When the bridge is glued to the soundboard it will overlap the lacquer slightly.

13 Before removing the rest of the masking tape, scrape off the sanding sealer and lightly coat the bridge area with a thin coat of glue. This will seal the wood and prevent the lacquer from sticking to the surface. Allow the glue to go tacky, then remove the remaining tape, being careful not to lift any soundboard fibres.

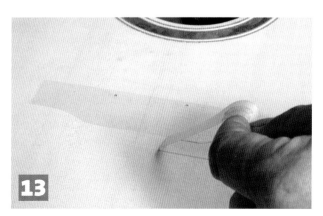

11 FINISHING

A smooth finish shows off the wood, and the workmanship, to best advantage

Acoustic and solid-body electric guitars have traditionally been finished in nitrocellulose lacquer, while nylon-strung classical and flamenco guitars are finished with shellac applied by the French-polishing method. Lacquer finish is much tougher than shellac, and the application and drying processes are more controllable for the factory set-up, while shellac needs to have an experienced hand to apply it, along with a great dollop of patience. We shall be using the lacquer method.

MATERIALS

- Woodstain as required
- Boiled linseed oil
- Turpentine
- Grain filler (see page 132)
- Nitrocellulose lacquer (see page 129)

THE WORKING AREA

Before we apply the finish we will need to set up the work area. The spraying area you require will depend on whether you are using a compressed-air system with a handheld spray gun, or just handheld aerosol cans, although in both cases the principles of environmental control are the same.

There are a few days in the year when the outside temperature is perfect and there is little or no wind; at these times you can do your spraying outside, provided you watch out for the washing line and drying clothes.

When I first started building guitars I used to have to spray in the main workshop, which sometimes prevented other work being done due to the smell of drying lacquer and the risk of contaminating the drying surface with airborne dust. French polishing using shellac was also done in the main workshop, with the same limitations. I did have a small fan to expel the fumes out of an open window.

Now I have a dedicated spray booth (see page 23) in another part of my external workshop. This booth is painted with white emulsion (latex) paint

WARNING

Most commercial French polishes use industrial thinners to dissolve the shellac, not drinking alcohol. When working with any solvents, wear a breathing mask suitable for organic gases.

once a month to cover the lacquer overspray. It is lined with 1in (25mm) plasterboard and lit with fluorescent lights. The roof is triplex plastic, which allows natural daylight to shine through, and it is fitted with a 3-speed extraction fan, with the controls outside the booth.

PREPARATION

1 Now down to work. Sand the whole body, starting with the dark woods, and being careful not to rub through on the edges at the purfling.

I start with 80-grit paper to lightly clean up the body sides and back after the purfling and binding are complete, then move to 150-grit to get rid of the scratches left by the 80-grit. I stay off the soundboard at this stage. Next, 400-grit wet & dry is used dry to bring up the grain and show up any spots where surplus glue might be lurking, especially adjacent to the binding and purfling. Finish with 800-grit.

Rubbing down the body with white spirit (mineral spirit) thinners will remove a lot of the surface dust and show you the colour and depth of the grain pattern of the wood, probably for the first time – I sometimes wipe down a few times as I am in awe of the beauty of the wood. With hardwoods that have a heavy oil content, such as the rosewoods, you need to be careful not to pull too much of the wood oil to the surface, as this will make it harder to rub down and will stain the lighter woods in the purfling.

1

LACQUERS AND SPRAY SYSTEMS

The simplest solution is the aerosol can of cellulose lacquer from the auto-parts shop. This will give you a fast build, and the nozzle will provide a suitable spray pattern for an object the size and shape of a guitar; more expensive cans will have a spray-pattern adjuster on the nozzle, which allows a choice of vertical or horizontal spray patterns. I used this method at first, and it used to take about four to five cans to cover a guitar, depending on how vigorous I was with the sanding between coats.

If you decide to invest in a professional compressor-driven system, then you will need a trade-rated machine. Mine is driven by a 1½hp motor, which delivers 9 cu ft per minute of air at a maximum air pressure of 114psi. The air tank holds 50 litres (11 gallons UK, 13 gallons US) of air, which is sufficient to spray guitars all day without running short of compressed air.

Lacquer is available as a one-part liquid that is thinned to the desired viscosity with the manufacturer's recommended thinners; the main drawback of this type is the long hardening time, sometimes as much as eight weeks at the colder times of year. Pre-catalysed lacquer will harden more quickly, but is more toxic to use. A third type is acid-catalysed lacquer, which has a catalyst added to aid curing; this is also toxic if not used in accordance with the manufacturer's instructions. Beyond lacquer, there are polyurethane two-part systems, and water-based lacquers are becoming more available. If unsure, consult a reputable trade paint retailer.

I have three sprayguns: an airbrush for touch-ups when repairing, a larger touch-up gun that sprays a pattern about 2in (50mm) wide, and a main gun that I refer to as my 'fire hose', as it can spray a soundboard in four passes when wide open.

2 Carefully scrape the binding and purfling clean to bring out the brightness of the lighter wood.

3 At an earlier stage we applied a coat of sanding sealer to the soundboard. Now is the time to remove it. Sand in the direction of the grain, starting with clean 150-grit paper, and working up to 800-grit to make sure that there are no scratches visible on the soundboard. Sanding over the glued area of the bridge will not do it any harm. Scrape the bindings, purfling and soundhole inlay clean as before. Sand the edge of the soundhole to a radius equal to half the thickness of the soundboard and backing plate.

4 Any small gaps between parts can be filled with a mixture of sawdust and superglue, applied with a spatula and scraped flush when set.

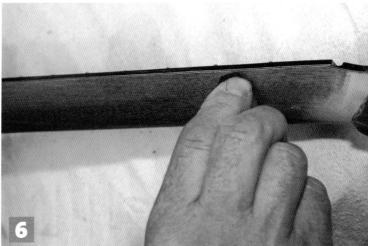

5 Paint all the inlays with one coat of blond lacquer; this seals the bright wood to prevent the grain filler from darkening it.

6 I like to stain the mahogany neck to match the much darker rosewood body. Experiment on offcuts of the neck wood to find the most suitable shade, then apply the colour with a folded rag. If you want a more 'antique' appearance, allow the stain to linger a little longer on the heel and blend its darker shade with the lighter neck; this can be done at the head as well. Don't make the stain too dark, or the neck colour will look muddy. Use masking tape if necessary to protect the ribs at the heel.

7 When complete, stain the whole guitar with a mixture of 50% boiled linseed oil and 50% turpentine. This is the moment when you start to see the real beauty of what you have created. Let the guitar hang in a well-ventilated area for a week to dry thoroughly.

Prepare for spraying by masking off the fretboard, working the masking tape tightly round the profile of the frets as you go, and filling the soundhole with crumpled newspaper to keep out the overspray. Spray three light coats of lacquer onto the soundboard and leave to dry completely. This will prevent it being contaminated by the grain filler.

WARNING

The rags that were used in the staining operation are a fire hazard. Store them in a lidded metal container until you are able to dispose of them safely.

WARNING

Before spraying, refer back to the safety precautions listed on page 25.

Use a suitable respirator, rated for organic fumes, and an extractor fan

USING A SPRAYGUN

Read the instructions supplied with your spraygun and take particular note of any safety advice. Some manufacturers state that the air hose should be conductive and earth-bonded to prevent the build-up of static electricity, which could cause an explosion in the event of a spark. The air supply must be dry and filtered; I have an inline water trap that changes colour when saturated.

Before you do any spraying, practise on a piece of plywood roughly the shape of the guitar. Start by mixing your lacquer and adding a small amount to the cup on the gun. Following the gun manufacturer's recommendations for air pressure, adjust the air and fluid valves. Hold the gun perpendicular to the work at a distance of about 6–8in (150–200mm). Start at the edge of the work and, keeping the gun perpendicular, spray across at a constant rate – finger off the trigger at the end of the pass, then back on again for the return pass. Overcoat the edge by half the width of the spray pattern. If the finish looks dry and dusty, try reducing the airflow; if the lacquer puddles, turn down the fluid-flow valve. With a little practice you will become quite proficient in a short time. An auto repair shop might be willing to give you a couple of lessons, if there is some favour you can do them in return.

There are several extremely good books on spraying guitars available from luthier suppliers. These cover the basics of preparation and mixing colours, as well as advanced techniques such as sunburst effects.

8 The hardwoods of the body and neck will need to have their pores filled with a suitable grain filler. You can buy a proprietary filler close in colour to the wood you are filling, or you can make your own as you go along – and it will be an exact colour match.

MATERIALS

For grain filler:
- Blond, de-waxed shellac
- Methylated spirit (denatured alcohol)
- Pumice powder
- Pumice bag
- French-polishing rubber

Make a pumice bag from an old, threadbare piece of cloth, filled with pumice powder. Lay the guitar face down on the bench, with a piece of carpet or similar underneath to protect the soundboard. Pour a little shellac onto the wood, and then shake the pumice over the shellac. Taking your French-polishing rubber, start working in a circular motion to rub the mix of pumice and polish into the grain of the wood. If it is too thick or dries out too quickly, add some methylated spirit (denatured alcohol) to the sludge. Keep working in circles; the pumice creates micro-sawdust that combines with the pumice and shellac to create the perfect colour-matched filler, and the circular action drags the filler into the pores of the wood. This is another of those jobs that should be practised beforehand on a piece of scrap wood.

When you are satisfied that the pores are filled, wipe the surplus filler off across the grain, then set the guitar aside for the shellac to dry. You may have to go through this process more than once to ensure that the pores are completely filled.

When dry, rub down in the direction of the grain with some steel wool, finishing with 400-grit sandpaper, using water if necessary to remove any gummy residue. You may have to scrape the purfling again to bring out the light-coloured wood.

APPLYING THE LACQUER

ORDER OF WORK
1 Soundboard
2 Back, neck, back and sides of head
3 Ribs and heel

9 With the materials I use, the soundboard needs about seven coats of lacquer, until a solid, flat surface appears after rubbing down. The rest of the body and neck take about ten coats. Lacquers in aerosol cans purchased from different suppliers will vary in viscosity, so with this method it is hard to predict how many coats will be required.

Lightly sand after the third coat, then after every two coats, till the lacquer takes a matt, flat finish when sanded. Then spray a final coat of thinned lacquer and leave the guitar hanging in a well-ventilated area for up to five weeks to dry completely.

When sanding near the edges, be careful not to rub through the finish. I start with 400-grit wet & dry, going down in stages to 1500-grit to attain an even, flat, matt appearance; always sand in the direction of the grain.

10 Now comes what could be the hard part of finishing: the polishing of the body to a high shine. Remove all masking tape on the fretboard before rubbing down. There are three methods of polishing. The first is by hand, with an automotive rubbing compound and a lint-free cotton cloth, which can give excellent results. The second is with a commercial automotive polisher; although powerful enough to do an excellent job, it is very heavy and cumbersome unless held in suspension by springs and cables, as is done in some factories. The third option is a bench-mounted professional polishing machine.

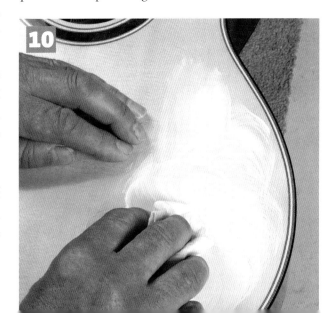

12 FINAL STAGES

All that remains, once the finish has thoroughly cured, is to fit the parts to which the strings are attached – the bridge and saddle, the nut and the machine tuners – and to make the final adjustments to the string action.

MATERIALS

- Bone for saddle, $4\frac{1}{4}$ x $\frac{15}{32}$ x $\frac{25}{64}$in (108 x 12 x 10mm)
- Machine tuners (see pages 38–9)
- Strings

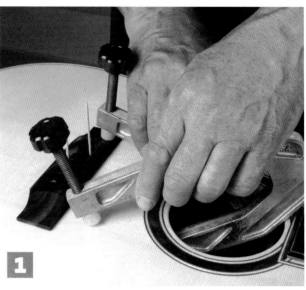

1

ATTACHING THE BRIDGE

1 An ebony bridge looks great when it is hand-polished with wax before being glued to the guitar. Carefully scrape any remaining masking-tape adhesive from the bridge area of the soundboard. Rough-sand the bridge area, being careful not to scratch the lacquer on the soundboard. Glue the two short $\frac{1}{16}$in (1.5mm) locating dowels into the holes previously drilled. Press the bridge down onto the dowels; the fit needs to be snug, but not so tight that the bridge will not lift off again.

2 If you have not already done so, refer to the plans and make the internal bridge-clamping caul, which bears against the bridge plate. To hold the caul in place during the gluing set-up, try wrapping a couple of turns of PVC electricians' tape around it with the sticky side out.

The finished guitar

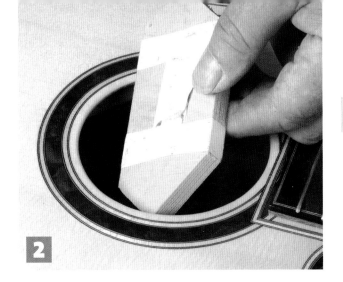

2

3 Do a dry run with the clamps and caul to ensure that everything is in order. Inserting the bridge clamps through the soundhole is a bit awkward; you might like to tape a piece of card over the soundboard to prevent scratching. Cut the locating dowels short so that they will not impinge on the saddle slot, and round their tops into a slight point to aid the positioning of the bridge.

Reach into the body of the guitar and press the caul into place. Insert the clamps and adjust them in readiness for clamping; leave them over to the side for now, keeping the bridge area clear.

Now apply glue to the bridge and firmly press it down into position. I use yellow glue (aliphatic resin) for this critical joint. Fit the clamps against the inner caul, and, with small cauls made from thin plywood placed under the clamp pads, gently tighten. Wipe up the glue squeeze-out with a slightly damp cloth, but be careful with this – if the cloth is too wet there is a risk of diluting the glue adjacent to the edge, causing a glue-starved joint. Use a shaped skewer to clean out all the remaining glue from the corners.

When the glue is thoroughly set, remove the clamps and cauls and do a final clean-up. I used to apply masking tape around the bridge area before gluing, but have come to the conclusion that this is not necessary, because any remaining glue will be in a smudgy film around the bridge, which can be cleaned up with a soft, clean, damp cloth.

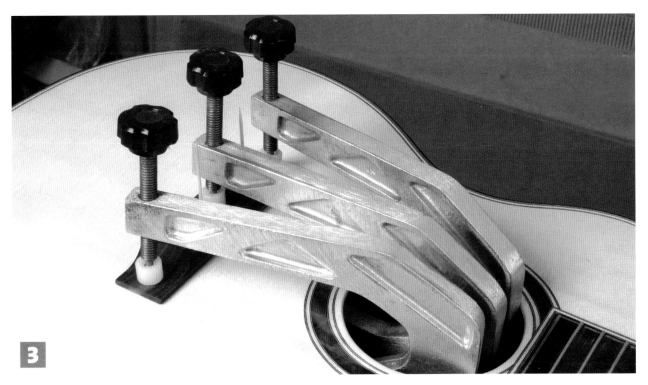

3

4 & 5 Drill out the holes for the bridge pins to a diameter of ³⁄₁₆in (5mm), then ream them to the same taper as the pins. You might like to try this operation on a scrap piece of timber first, to get the feel of reaming the hole and trying the fit of a bridge pin. There should be a slight gap, say ¹⁄₁₆in (1.5mm), between the underside of the ball end on the pin and the top of the bridge; this aids in removing the pin when changing strings.

TIP

If you are only making one instrument and do not want to invest in a purpose-made reamer, the tapering can be done with the tang of a file.

The top of the pin hole needs to be slightly chamfered so that the strings are not tensioned against a sharp corner. If you have not already done so, use a countersink to break the edge, leaving a margin of about ¹⁄₃₂in (1mm).

A small groove needs to be cut down the front side of each hole for the ends of the strings to rest in. I do this with a tight-radius jigsaw blade held in a small handle made from an offcut of rosewood. The width of each groove needs to be slightly more than the diameter of the wound end of the string.

THE SADDLE

6 Now take the bone saddle, cut it to the same length as the slot in the bridge, and round over the ends to match. Sand with progressively finer grades of wet & dry paper, ending with 800-grit, until it fits the slot. It should be a tight fit, although still able to be removed. The top is shaped to match the curvature of the fretboard, but set the treble side about ¹⁄₃₂in (1mm) lower than the bass side, to allow for the reduced diameters of the upper strings. Draw the radius so that it touches the top edge of the saddle, using the same gauge as was used for the fretboard. Sand down to this line; I use a drum sander held in the pillar drill. Finish by sanding the radius with 220-grit wet & dry paper.

7 After sanding, the saddle should have no rough or angular surfaces to catch on the strings.

STRING GAUGES

Each string has different diameter: the E string on the treble side is the smallest, and the E on the bass side is the largest. EL (extra-light) strings are easier to play but will not project as much sound as L (light) or M (medium-gauge) strings.

THE NUT

8&9 Next fit the top nut and mark the width; remove, trim to width and replace. Take a pencil and sand one face flat, down to and including the lead. Lay this pencil lead-side down on top of the frets and draw a line along the face of the top nut. Remove the nut and file or sand down to about ⁵⁄₆₄in (2mm) above the line.

10 Before you can work the string slots in the top nut you will require some nut files, which can be either flat or round. These are available from luthier suppliers, in varying widths to match the string widths. They are not cheap, but will make the job a lot easier. Prepare by placing the guitar on the bench with the neck to your left (if you are right-handed).

First set the spacing of the strings at the top nut, then the height of the strings over the frets. Mark the nut ⅛in (3mm) in from the edge on both sides. Then divide the space in between into five equal intervals; this gives the positions of the other four strings. Alternatively, there are proprietary rulers for marking string positions on the top nut. File small grooves into the nut, just deep enough to hold the strings in place at this stage.

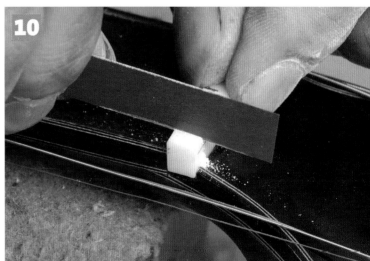

MACHINE TUNERS

11 The individual tuners used on most steel-string guitars are easy to fit: the main body of the tuner is passed through the head from the back, then the washer and string post are threaded on from the front. If the lacquer has slightly reduced the diameter of the holes in the head, a kiss with the reamer is all that is needed to clean the edges. A small screw is inserted through the lug at the back to prevent the tuner from rotating out of alignment as the string is tensioned. The tuners are arranged so that those on the bass side turn anticlockwise (as seen from the front) to tighten the strings, and those on the treble side turn clockwise.

SETTING UP

12 Now fit the strings and tighten them till they are straight and taut, but not tuned up to pitch. The outermost strings should be almost parallel to the edge of the neck, but moving slightly further in as you go up the fretboard.

With all the strings taut and in place, depress each string in turn between the second and third frets, and look at the clearance at the first fret. The height of the strings above the frets – known as the *action* – will determine the playability of the guitar.

FITTING STRINGS

Start with the bass E string. Push the ball end through the pin hole in the bridge, push the string into its groove and insert the bridge pin lightly. Gently pull back on the string. If you reach inside the guitar you can feel whether the ball end of the string has seated itself against the underside of the bridge plate; when satisfied that it has, gently press the bridge pin down. Take the end of the string and feed it through the hole in the machine tuner, leaving a slack bow of guitar string lying on the fretboard. Gently trap the string in the tuner with your fingers and start to tighten, remembering the correct direction of rotation for each string. The bass E string goes to the tuner closest to the top nut on the bass side, the A string goes to the middle tuner and the D to the furthest tuner. The other three strings are fitted in the reverse order on the treble side of the head, finishing with the treble E string, which goes to the tuner closest to the top nut on that side.

The lower the strings are, generally speaking, the easier the guitar will be to play; however, too low and the strings will buzz on the frets. The thicker strings should have about $\frac{1}{32}$in (1mm) extra clearance at the 14th fret to prevent them buzzing. These adjustments are made when the saddle is given its final shaping.

Slacken off all except the treble E string. Gently pull the treble strings over to the treble side of the nut and the bass strings to the bass side. Start by pressing the E string down between the second and third frets, and look horizontally at the gap between the underside of the string and the top of the crown of the fret. If the nut slot has been adjusted to its ideal depth you will end up with a very small gap between the string and the first fret – about 0.006in (0.15mm). If you're not sure whether there is a gap under the string, try tapping lightly on the string close to the first fret, with the string pressed down between the second and third frets; if the gap is present you will hear a metallic sound as the string makes contact with the fret. Gently lift the string out of its position and start filing the slot, frequently placing the string back in its notch and, with the string depressed between the second and third frets, measuring the first-fret gap with a feeler gauge.

When the first string is done, move on to the next, and continue till all the strings are seated at the correct height. The wound strings should sit with half their diameter in the slots, and the two highest strings should be flush with the top of the nut. When complete, the bottom of the slot should have a radius and the strings should not be so tight that they jam in position, nor so loose that they make a sound like a sitar as they vibrate in the slot. When you have completed the remaining strings, remove the nut and sand the top of it till the slots for the wound strings are just semicircular, while those for the top two strings are equal in depth to the string diameters. The top edge of the nut, for a distance of about ⅛in (3mm) on the head side, needs to be bevelled back at about 14° so that the top surface is parallel to the front of the head. Once all shaping is finished, repolish the top of the nut and refit it. The nut does not need to be glued, but some luthiers place a drop of glue on the underside

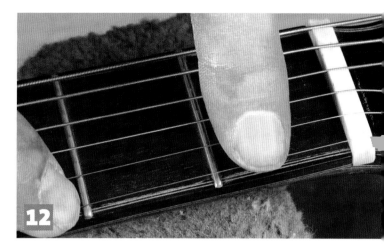

of the nut just to prevent it from creeping sideways when the player changes to altered tunings during a performance.

To set the action at the bridge end, we start by measuring the string gap at the 12th fret. A suitable height is about $\frac{5}{32}$in (4mm) on the sixth string, decreasing to ⅛in (3mm) at the first string. There are no notches in the saddle; simply file down each section till you have the desired gap between string and fret. When all the strings are done, refile the radius on the top of the saddle, blending it into the curve on the end, and use wet & dry paper to round over the top so it cannot snag the strings. Now all you have to do is tune the strings up to pitch, trim off the excess length, and play.

TEETHING PROBLEMS

As you begin to play your new guitar you may hear the occasional buzz. There are two likely causes: either one fret is slightly higher than the others, or the ball end of a string is vibrating against a bridge pin. Picking each string slowly and gently while working your way up the fretboard should determine if it is a fret. If it is just one fret on a single string, this can be eased by filing with the crowning file, then repolishing the fret. If this does not locate the problem, it could be one of the ball ends. Slacken off the string, partially pull out the bridge pin and gently tug on the string till the end is properly seated, then reinsert the pin and tune up.

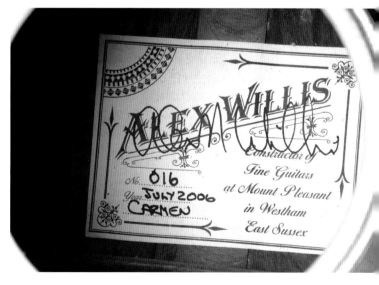

Don't be afraid to celebrate your achievement by designing a suitable label

abalone a marine shell sometimes used for inlay decoration.

ablam an artificial inlay material consisting of reconstituted abalone shards cast in epoxy resin.

action the height of the strings over the frets.

ball end a metal fitting wound onto the bridge end of the string to prevent it from pulling out of its hole.

bass side the side of the instrument where the lowest-pitch strings are located.

binding a hardwood strip fitted to the edges of the guitar body to protect the end grain of the soundboard and back.

bookmatching cutting a piece of wood in half through its thickness and joining the resulting pieces to produce a symmetrical grain pattern.

bouts (upper and lower) the two widest parts of the guitar body, above and below the waist.

braces the timbers glued to the inside of the soundboard and back to strengthen them; those on the soundboard are sometimes called **tone bars**. For the names of individual braces, see page 13.

bridge the bar to which the strings are anchored on the soundboard.

bridge pin the tapered pin that retains the string in its hole in the bridge.

bridge plate a reinforcing piece glued to the underside of the soundboard in the bridge area, for the ball ends of the strings to pull against.

burr (burl) a section of timber cut from the root of a tree, usually highly figured.

cutaway an incurved section in the treble-side rib of some guitars, next to the neck, to enable the player to reach the top end of the fretboard more easily.

endblock a wooden block glued inside the body at the lower end, providing attachment for the ribs, soundboard and back.

figure any decorative pattern which occurs naturally in a piece of wood, resulting from the lie of the grain and other natural features.

fret a metal bar fixed into the **fretboard** on the front surface of the neck, against which the string is pressed (or 'stopped') to produce a specific note.

head the top end of the guitar neck, where the tuners are attached.

heel the root of the neck, where it joins the body.

heel cap a decorative pad fixed to the underside of the heel to make it flush with the back of the guitar.

intonation the accurate pitching of a musical note.

kerfing a series of transverse slits which may be cut into the linings to help them bend to the curvature of the body,

as an alternative to the heat-bending technique described in this book.

linings narrow strips of timber attached to the inside edges of the ribs to increase the gluing surface when the soundboard and back are attached.

machine tuner or **tuning head** a geared metal device for adjusting the tension of the guitar string.

MOP marine shell cut into small, irregular four-sided sections for inlay decoration.

nut a grooved block of bone or other hard material fitted to the top end of the fretboard to hold the strings at the correct height and spacing.

purfling decorative veneer strips inlaid around the perimeter of the guitar body.

quartersawing cutting wood so that the grain is perpendicular to the surface.

ribs the two bent pieces of wood which form the sides of the guitar body.

rosette the decorative ring inlaid around the soundhole.

saddle the ridge of bone or other hard material fitted into the bridge for the strings to ride over.

scale length the nominal vibrating length of the strings, disregarding any extra amount added at the bridge to compensate for the stretching of the strings as they are stopped against the frets (see page 126).

slipper block the part of the neck that extends into the body and is glued to the guitar back, in the method of construction adopted in this book.

solera the baseboard on which the guitar is assembled, in the construction method used in this book.

soundboard the front plate of the guitar body, which serves to amplify the vibration of the strings.

soundhole the usually circular opening in the soundboard, normally placed on the centre line between the fretboard and the bridge.

string gauge the diameter of a string, usually measured in thousands of an inch or in decimal points of a millimetre.

stump wood decorative wood cut from the stumps of exotic trees, especially Brazilian rosewood, which can be used for guitar backs and sides.

tonewood any wood of suitable quality to be used in the making of musical instruments.

treble side the side of the instrument where the highest-pitched strings are located.

truss rod the metal rod installed in the neck of most steel-string guitars to help keep the fretboard flat under string tension.

waist the narrowest part of the guitar body.

CONVERSION TABLE

in	mm	in	mm	in	mm	in	mm
1/64	0.3969	31/64	12.3031	15/16	23.8125	5	127.000
1/32	0.7937	1/2	12.7000	61/64	24.2094	6	152.400
3/64	1.1906			31/32	24.6062	7	177.800
1/16	1.5875	33/64	13.0969	63/64	25.0031	8	203.200
5/64	1.9844	17/32	13.4937	1	25.4001	9	228.600
3/32	2.3812	35/64	13.8906			10	254.001
7/64	2.7781	9/16	14.2875	1 1/8	28.5751	11	279.401
1/8	3.1750	37/64	14.6844	1 1/4	31.7501	12	304.801
		19/32	15.0812	1 3/8	34.9251	13	330.201
9/64	3.5719	39/64	15.4781	1 1/2	38.1001	14	355.601
5/32	3.9687	5/8	15.8750	1 5/8	41.2751	15	381.001
11/64	4.3656			1 3/4	44.4501	16	406.401
3/16	4.7625	41/64	16.2719	1 7/8	47.6251	17	431.801
13/64	5.1594	21/32	16.6687	2	50.8001	18	457.201
7/32	5.5562	43/64	17.0656			19	482.601
15/64	5.9531	11/16	17.4625	2 1/8	53.9751	20	508.001
1/4	6.3500	45/64	17.8594	2 1/4	57.1501	21	533.401
		23/32	18.2562	2 3/8	60.3251	22	558.801
17/64	6.7469	47/64	18.6531	2 1/2	63.5001	23	584.201
9/32	7.1437	3/4	19.0500	2 5/8	66.6751	24	609.601
19/64	7.5406			2 3/4	69.8501		
5/16	7.9375	49/64	19.4469	2 7/8	73.0251	25	635.001
21/64	8.3344	25/32	19.8437	3	76.2002	26	660.401
11/32	8.7312	51/64	20.2406			27	685.801
23/64	9.1281	13/16	20.6375			28	711.201
3/8	9.5250	53/64	21.0344	3 1/8	79.3752	29	736.601
		27/32	21.4312	3 1/4	82.5502	30	762.002
25/64	9.9219	55/64	21.8281	3 3/8	85.7252	31	787.402
13/32	10.3187	7/8	22.2250	3 1/2	88.9002	32	812.802
27/64	10.7156			3 5/8	92.0752	33	838.202
7/16	11.1125	57/64	22.6219	3 3/4	95.2502	34	863.602
29/64	11.5094	29/32	23.0187	3 7/8	98.4252	35	889.002
15/32	11.9062	59/64	23.4156	4	101.500	36	914.402

FRET POSITIONS

Distance from the face of the nut to the centre of each fret, for a scale length of 25.52in (648mm)

Fret no.	in	mm	Fret no.	in	mm
1	1.43	36.37	12	12.76	324.00
2	2.78	70.70	13	13.47	342.19
3	4.06	103.10	14	14.15	359.35
4	5.26	133.68	15	14.79	375.55
5	6.40	162.55	16	15.39	390.84
6	7.47	189.80	17	15.96	405.28
7	8.48	215.51	18	16.49	418.90
8	9.44	239.79	19	17.00	431.76
9	10.34	262.70	20	17.48	443.89
10	11.19	284.32	21	17.93	455.35
11	12.00	304.74	22	18.35	466.16

ABOUT THE AUTHOR

When Alex Willis was about five years old he visited his grandparents at Port Glasgow, Scotland, and the constant sound of riveting from the Clydeside shipyards gave him a subliminal desire to build a boat. This would eventually lead him (after spending some time in the Royal Navy) to building boats in sunny California, where he met his future wife Nancy; and the first boat he built became their home for the next 11 years. At the age of 43 he returned to live permanently in the UK with his wife and their three children, Stephen, Stephanie and Sandra,

and opened a business designing and installing computer networks.

Unable to get a boat into his small garden workshop, at the behest of classical guitar-playing friends Rob and Gilly he decided to learn about making guitars; Roy Courtnall's excellent book *Making Master Guitars* was his guide. In 2003 he made the decision to devote his time to guitar design, construction and repair. The greatest joy for him is to hand a brand-new guitar to its new owner and hear it come to life for the first time.
www.willisguitars.co.uk

RESOURCES

USA

Allied Lutherie
www.alliedlutherie.com
Luthiers' tools and materials

Elderly Instruments
www.elderly.com
Musical instruments, spares and books.

Luthiers' Mercantile International, Inc.
www.lmii.com
Luthiers' tools, materials and books

Stewart-MacDonald
www.stewmac.com
Luthiers' tools, materials and books

Woodcraft
www.woodcraft.com
Luthiers' tools, materials and books

UK

Ashley Mark Publishing Company
www.ashleymark.co.uk
All books on music

Axminster Power Tool Centre Ltd
www.axminster.co.uk
Tools and books
Craft Supplies Ltd
www.craft-supplies.co.uk
Luthiers' tools, materials and books

David Dyke Luthiers' Supplies
www.luthierssupplies.co.uk
Luthiers' tools, materials and books

Hiscox Cases Ltd
www.hiscoxcases.com
Custom-made instrument cases

Small Wonder Music
www.smallwonder-music.co.uk
Shell and alternative materials for inlaying; specialized tools

Timberline
www.exotichardwoods.co.uk
Luthiers' tools, materials and books

Touchstone Tonewoods
www.touchstonetonewoods.co.uk
Luthiers' tools, materials and books

EUROPE

Dick GmbH
www.dick-gmbh.de (website in German and English)
Luthiers' tools and books

Ets Kauffer
www.kauffer.com (website in French and English)
Luthiers' materials

INDEX

GMC Publications, Castle Place, 166 High Street, Lewes, East Sussex BN7 1XU, United Kingdom
Tel: 01273 488005 Fax: 01273 402866
E-mail: pubs@thegmcgroup.com Website: www.gmcbooks.com
Contact us for a complete catalogue, or visit our website. Orders by credit card are accepted.